First World War
and Army of Occupation
War Diary
France, Belgium and Germany

3 DIVISION
Divisional Troops
Royal Army Veterinary Corps
11 Mobile Veterinary Section
5 August 1914 - 27 October 1919

WO95/1408/3

The Naval & Military Press Ltd
www.nmarchive.com
Published in association with The National Archives

Published by

The Naval & Military Press Ltd

Unit 10 Ridgewood Industrial Park,
Uckfield, East Sussex,
TN22 5QE England
Tel: +44 (0) 1825 749494

www.naval-military-press.com
www.nmarchive.com

This diary has been reprinted in facsimile from the original. Any imperfections are inevitably reproduced and the quality may fall short of modern type and cartographic standards.

Contents

Document type	Place/Title	Date From	Date To
Heading	WO95/1408/3		
Heading	3rd Division Divl. Troops 11th Mobile Vety Section 1914 Aug-1919 Oct		
Heading	3rd Div, 11th M.V.S., War Diary, Aug-Dec., 1914		
Heading	121/1363 3rd Div. No 11 Mobile Veterinary Section Vol I Aug 1914		
War Diary	Woolwich	05/08/1914	19/08/1914
War Diary	Southampton	20/08/1914	20/08/1914
War Diary	Harve	21/08/1914	21/08/1914
War Diary	Rouen	22/08/1914	25/08/1914
War Diary	St Quentin	26/08/1914	26/08/1914
War Diary	Harve	27/08/1914	27/08/1914
War Diary	Sempigny	27/08/1914	29/08/1914
War Diary	Compeigne	29/08/1914	30/08/1914
War Diary	La Vache Noire	31/08/1914	31/08/1914
Heading	121/2165 No 11 Mobile Vety Section Volume II 1-30.9.14		
War Diary	?Vancimutes	01/09/1914	01/09/1914
War Diary	Villers-St-Genest	02/09/1914	02/09/1914
War Diary	Meant	03/09/1914	03/09/1914
War Diary	La Haute Maison	04/09/1914	04/09/1914
War Diary	Marles	05/09/1914	05/09/1914
War Diary	Chatres	06/09/1914	06/09/1914
War Diary	Grevecoeur	07/09/1914	07/09/1914
War Diary	Hamfemile	08/09/1914	08/09/1914
War Diary	Marles	09/09/1914	09/09/1914
War Diary	Saoray	10/09/1914	10/09/1914
War Diary	Chezy-En-Orxois	11/09/1914	11/09/1914
War Diary	Grand Rozoy	12/09/1914	12/09/1914
War Diary	Cerseuil	13/09/1914	13/09/1914
War Diary	Braine	14/09/1914	14/09/1914
War Diary	Cuiry House	15/09/1914	16/09/1914
War Diary	Fave-en-Tardeous	17/09/1914	17/09/1914
War Diary	Vichel-Nanteuil	18/09/1914	19/09/1914
War Diary	Curney House	20/09/1914	21/09/1914
War Diary	Braine	22/09/1914	30/09/1914
Heading	121/1363 No 11 Mobile Veterinary Section Vol II Sept 1914		
War Diary	Villiers S. Genesie	01/09/1914	01/09/1914
War Diary	Monthyon	02/09/1914	02/09/1914
War Diary	La Haute Maison	03/09/1914	04/09/1914
War Diary	Chatres	05/09/1914	06/09/1914
War Diary	Hautefeuille	07/09/1914	07/09/1914
War Diary	Bussieres	08/09/1914	08/09/1914
War Diary	Bezu Le Guery	09/09/1914	09/09/1914
War Diary	Coulomiers	10/09/1914	10/09/1914
War Diary	Montreuil	11/09/1914	11/09/1914
War Diary	Vichel	12/09/1914	12/09/1914
War Diary	Cury House	13/09/1914	14/09/1914
War Diary	Braine	14/09/1914	30/09/1914

Heading	121/1967 11 Mobile Vety Sector Vol III 1-31.10.14		
War Diary	Braine	01/10/1914	03/10/1914
War Diary	Arcy	03/10/1914	03/10/1914
War Diary	La Ferte Milon	04/10/1914	04/10/1914
War Diary	Crepy En Valois	05/10/1914	05/10/1914
War Diary	Abbeville	06/10/1914	09/10/1914
War Diary	Labroye	10/10/1914	10/10/1914
War Diary	Pernes	11/10/1914	13/10/1914
War Diary	Zelobes	14/10/1914	17/10/1914
War Diary	Pernes	18/10/1914	18/10/1914
War Diary	Zelobes	19/10/1914	19/10/1914
War Diary	Pont Logy	20/10/1914	21/10/1914
War Diary	Vieille Chapelle	22/10/1914	27/10/1914
War Diary	Lapugnoy	28/10/1914	29/10/1914
War Diary	Lestrem	30/10/1914	31/10/1914
Heading	121/2599 No 11 Mobile Veterinary Section Vol IV		
War Diary	Lestrem	01/11/1914	07/11/1914
War Diary	Moolenacker	08/11/1914	09/11/1914
War Diary	Lestrem	10/11/1914	15/11/1914
War Diary	Merville	16/11/1914	16/11/1914
War Diary	Meteren	17/11/1914	19/11/1914
War Diary	Berthen	20/11/1914	30/11/1914
Heading	121/3944 3rd Division No 11 Mobile Vety Sect Vol V 1-31.12.14		
War Diary	Berthen	01/12/1914	31/12/1914
Heading	3rd Div, 11th Mobile Vety Section War Diary Jan-Dec., 1915		
Heading	3rd Division 11th Mobile Vety Section Vol VI Jan 1915		
War Diary	Berthen	01/01/1915	31/01/1915
Heading	121/4559 3rd Division No 11 Mobile Veterinary Section Vol VII Feb 1914		
War Diary	Berthen	01/02/1915	28/02/1915
Heading	121/4779 3rd Division 11th Mobile Vety Section Vol VIII March 1915		
War Diary	Berthen	01/03/1915	31/03/1915
Heading	121/5194 3rd Division 11th Mobile Vety Section Vol IX 1-30.4.15		
War Diary	Bethun	01/04/1915	15/04/1915
War Diary	Westoutre	15/04/1915	30/04/1915
Heading	121/5481 3rd Division No 11 Mobile Vety Section Vol X 1-31.5.15		
War Diary	At. Hestenhe	01/05/1915	31/05/1915
Heading	121/5993 3rd Division No 11 Mobile Vety Section Vol XI 1-30.6.15		
War Diary	At Hestentes	01/06/1915	05/06/1915
War Diary	Poperinghe	06/06/1915	30/06/1915
Heading	121/6243 3rd Division No 11 Mobile Vety Section Vol XII 1-31-4-15		
War Diary	Poperinghe	01/07/1915	31/07/1915
Heading	121/6607 3rd Division No 11 Mobile Vety Section Vol XIII From 1-31.8.15		
War Diary	Poperinghe	01/08/1915	31/08/1915
Heading	121/7051 3rd Division No 11 Mobile Vety Section Vol XIV Sept 15		
War Diary	Poperinghe	01/09/1915	30/09/1915
Heading	121/7929 3rd Div 11th Mob. Vet. Sec. Oct Vol XIV		

War Diary	In The Field	01/10/1915	01/10/1915
War Diary	At Popenighe	02/10/1915	23/10/1915
War Diary	Stenoonde	24/10/1915	31/10/1915
Heading	121/7662 3rd Division 11 Mobile Vet. Sec Nov Vol XVI		
War Diary	Stenoonde	01/11/1915	25/11/1915
War Diary	Westoutre	26/11/1915	30/11/1915
Heading	11th Mob. Vet. Sec Dec Vol XVII		
War Diary	Westoutre	01/12/1915	31/12/1915
War Diary	3rd Division Divl. Troops 11th Mobile Vety Section Jan-Dec 1916		
Heading	11th Mob. Vet. Sec. Jan Vol XVIII		
War Diary	At Westonthe	01/01/1916	16/01/1916
War Diary	Westoutre	17/01/1916	31/01/1916
Heading	11 Mobile Vety Sec Feb Vol XIX		
War Diary	Westoutre	01/02/1916	11/02/1916
War Diary	Wemaers-Cappel	12/02/1916	12/02/1916
War Diary	Nordausques	13/02/1916	29/02/1916
Heading	11 Mob Vety Sec Vol XX		
War Diary	Nordausques	01/03/1916	10/03/1916
War Diary	Wemaers Cappel	11/03/1916	11/03/1916
War Diary	Westoutre	12/03/1916	31/03/1916
Heading	11 Mob Vety Sect Vol XXI		
War Diary	Westoutre	01/04/1916	07/04/1916
War Diary	Fethe	08/04/1916	30/04/1916
War Diary	Westoutre	01/05/1916	30/05/1916
War Diary	Coyde Paille	31/05/1916	18/06/1916
War Diary	Wemaers Cappel	19/06/1916	19/06/1916
War Diary	Birkule	20/06/1916	20/06/1916
War Diary	Tilques	21/06/1916	30/06/1916
Miscellaneous	A.D.V.S. 3rd Division		
War Diary	Tilques	01/07/1916	01/07/1916
War Diary	Lanches	02/07/1916	02/07/1916
War Diary	Bettincourt	03/07/1916	04/07/1916
War Diary	Bertangles	05/07/1916	05/07/1916
War Diary	Lahoussye	06/07/1916	06/07/1916
War Diary	Bois-de-Taille	06/07/1916	07/07/1916
War Diary	Sailly-Le-Sec	07/07/1916	15/07/1916
War Diary	GroveTown	15/07/1916	28/07/1916
War Diary	Ville-Sur-Ancre	28/07/1916	16/08/1916
War Diary	GroveTown	16/08/1916	21/08/1916
War Diary	Treux	21/08/1916	22/08/1916
War Diary	Flesselles	22/08/1916	23/08/1916
War Diary	Bernaville	23/08/1916	25/08/1916
War Diary	Frohen-Le-Grand	25/08/1916	26/08/1916
War Diary	Flers	26/08/1916	27/08/1916
War Diary	Monchy Cayeux	27/08/1916	28/08/1916
War Diary	Noeux Les Mines	28/08/1916	24/09/1916
War Diary	La Pugnoye	24/09/1916	25/09/1916
War Diary	The Rouanne	25/09/1916	05/10/1916
War Diary	Teneur	05/10/1916	16/10/1916
War Diary	Berlencourt	06/10/1916	07/10/1916
War Diary	Bertrancourt	07/10/1916	09/10/1916
War Diary	Acheux	10/10/1916	18/10/1916
War Diary	B U S	19/10/1916	31/10/1916
War Diary	Bus-Les-Artois	01/11/1916	31/12/1916

Heading	3rd Division No. 11 Mobile Veterinary Section Jan-Dec 1917		
War Diary	Bus-Les-Artois	01/01/1917	07/01/1917
War Diary	Jus Les Aartois	08/01/1917	08/01/1917
War Diary	St Ouen	08/01/1917	29/01/1917
War Diary	Sarton	29/01/1917	30/01/1917
War Diary	Conchy-Sur-Canche	30/01/1917	01/02/1917
War Diary	La Comte	01/02/1917	08/02/1917
War Diary	Canettemont	08/02/1917	23/02/1917
War Diary	Avesnes-Le Comte	23/02/1917	01/04/1917
War Diary	Wanquetin	01/04/1917	11/04/1917
War Diary	Arras	11/04/1917	16/04/1917
War Diary	Dainville	16/04/1917	27/04/1917
War Diary	Arras	27/04/1917	15/05/1917
War Diary	Agnez	15/05/1917	19/05/1917
War Diary	Lignereuil	19/05/1917	02/06/1917
War Diary	Achicourt	02/06/1917	20/06/1917
War Diary	Le Cauroy	20/06/1917	30/06/1917
Heading	H.Q. (A) III Div		
War Diary	Halloy	01/07/1917	01/07/1917
War Diary	Bihucourt	01/07/1917	04/07/1917
War Diary	Bapaume	04/07/1917	08/09/1917
War Diary	Rocquigny	08/09/1917	15/09/1917
War Diary	Hopoutre	16/09/1917	16/09/1917
War Diary	Watou	16/09/1917	24/09/1917
War Diary	Poperinghe	24/09/1917	30/09/1917
War Diary	Sheet 28 G 14.C.5.4	01/10/1917	01/10/1917
War Diary	Sheet 27 J 18.C.7.7	02/10/1917	04/10/1917
War Diary	Renescure	05/10/1917	05/10/1917
War Diary	Condardenne	06/10/1917	06/10/1917
War Diary	Le Mesnil	07/10/1917	12/10/1917
War Diary	Favreuil	13/10/1917	15/12/1917
War Diary	Eruillers	16/12/1917	28/01/1918
War Diary	Boisleux-Au-Mont	29/01/1918	21/03/1918
War Diary	Grosville	22/03/1918	28/03/1918
War Diary	Gouy-En-Artois	29/03/1918	29/03/1918
War Diary	Lucheux	30/03/1918	31/03/1918
War Diary	Averdoingt	01/04/1918	01/04/1918
War Diary	Bruay	02/04/1918	04/04/1918
War Diary	Hesdigneul	05/04/1918	10/04/1918
War Diary	Busnetts	11/04/1918	11/04/1918
War Diary	Hurionville	12/04/1918	15/04/1918
War Diary	Bruay	16/04/1918	27/04/1918
War Diary	Bois De Dames	28/04/1918	06/08/1918
War Diary	Raimbert	07/08/1918	09/08/1918
War Diary	Auchel	10/08/1918	12/08/1918
War Diary	Anvin	13/08/1918	13/08/1918
War Diary	Humbercourt	14/08/1918	14/08/1918
War Diary	Bavincourt	15/08/1918	19/08/1918
War Diary	La Cauchie	20/08/1918	22/08/1918
War Diary	Monchy Au Bois	23/08/1918	27/08/1918
War Diary	Boiry St Rictrude	28/08/1918	06/09/1918
War Diary	Douchy	07/09/1918	12/09/1918
War Diary	Ervillers	13/09/1918	14/09/1918
War Diary	Vraucourt	15/09/1918	15/09/1918
War Diary	Vaulx-Vraucourt	16/09/1918	25/09/1918

War Diary	Le Bucquiere	26/09/1918	30/09/1918
War Diary	Hermies	01/10/1918	02/10/1918
War Diary	Havrincourt	03/10/1918	08/10/1918
War Diary	Hermies	09/10/1918	12/10/1918
War Diary	Ribecourt	13/10/1918	19/10/1918
War Diary	Wambaix	20/10/1918	21/10/1918
War Diary	Bevillers	22/10/1918	22/10/1918
War Diary	Solesmes	23/10/1918	25/10/1918
War Diary	Romeries	26/10/1918	31/10/1918
War Diary	Carniers	01/11/1918	04/11/1918
War Diary	Solesmes	05/11/1918	09/11/1918
War Diary	Frasnoy	10/11/1918	17/11/1918
War Diary	Sous-Les-Bois	18/11/1918	20/11/1918
War Diary	Rousies	21/11/1918	24/11/1918
War Diary	Solre-Sur-Sambre	25/11/1918	25/11/1918
War Diary	Marbaix	26/11/1918	27/11/1918
War Diary	Biesme	28/11/1918	28/11/1918
War Diary	St Gerard	29/11/1918	29/11/1918
War Diary	Yvoir	30/11/1918	30/11/1918
Miscellaneous	X M.V.S.		
War Diary	Yvoir	01/12/1918	04/12/1918
War Diary	Durnal	05/12/1918	05/12/1918
War Diary	Trisogne	06/12/1918	06/12/1918
War Diary	Baillomille	07/12/1918	07/12/1918
War Diary	Fronville	08/12/1918	08/12/1918
War Diary	Erezee	09/12/1918	10/12/1918
War Diary	Odegine	11/12/1918	11/12/1918
War Diary	Comte	12/12/1918	12/12/1918
War Diary	Beho	13/12/1918	13/12/1918
War Diary	Neundorf	14/12/1918	14/12/1918
War Diary	Schonberg	15/12/1918	15/12/1918
War Diary	Kronenburg	16/12/1918	16/12/1918
War Diary	Blankenhiem	17/12/1918	17/12/1918
War Diary	Mechenich	18/12/1918	18/12/1918
War Diary	Wollersheim	19/12/1918	19/12/1918
War Diary	Krauthsn	20/12/1918	31/12/1918
War Diary	Duren	01/01/1919	28/02/1919
War Diary	Kerpen	01/03/1919	02/03/1919
War Diary	Coln	03/03/1919	31/03/1919
War Diary	Cologne	01/07/1919	31/08/1919
War Diary	Coln	01/09/1919	27/10/1919

3RD DIVISION
DIVL. TROOPS

11TH MOBILE VETY SECTION
~~AUG 1914 TO~~
~~DEC 1918~~

1914 AUG — 1919 OCT

Index

SUBJECT.

No.	Contents.	Date.
	3RD DIV, — 11TH M.V.S., — WAR DIARY, AUG - DEC, 1914	

(56,425). Wt.24,741—161. 2000. 11/20. Gp.164. A.&E.W.

3rd Div.

121/1363

W.D

No. 11. Mobile Veterinary Section.

Vol. I.

Aug 1914

1

Army Form C. 2118.

Instructions regarding War Diaries and Intelligence Summaries are contained in F. S. Regs., Part II. and the Staff Manual respectively. Title pages will be prepared in manuscript.

WAR DIARY

~~or~~

~~INTELLIGENCE SUMMARY~~

(*Erase heading not required.*)

Hour, Date, Place			Summary of Events and Information	Remarks and References to Appendices
	5. 8. 14	Woolwich	Mobilization orders received.	
	6. 8. 14	do	Took over command of No XI Mobile Veterinary Section which was formed at Woolwich on mobilization	
	7 to 10. 8. 14	do	On duty at Horse collecting depôt, Well Hall Road. Unable to supervise the formation of the Mobile Section – Took over the Section horses at 5pm on 10th	
	11 to 18. 8. 14	do	Fitting and adjusting of harness, saddlery &c. Training horses which had been purchased on mobilization. Although I had taken over command of the section, the N.C.O's and men were not entirely under my control as they were continually being taken away by O.C. A.V.C. Woolwich for other duties. During this period I found that owing to not doing mounted duty in peace the majority of N.C.O's and men required a considerable amount of instruction in riding, saddle fitting &c.	
1.30 pm.	19. 8. 14.	do	Marched to West Croydon to entrain. Arrived 4.20pm Left 6.5pm Arrived Southampton 11.40 pm	
3.40 am	20 8. 14	Southampton	Embarked on S.S. Lord Charlemont. Sailed 9 am. Arrived off Havre 8 pm and anchored.	
7.0 am.	21. 8. 14.	Havre	Sailed 7 am. Arrived Rouen 3.40 pm. Disembarked by 5.30pm Marched to Bruyeres Rest Camp where I arrived at 9pm. Dark and found the one lantern as allowed insufficient.	
	22 to 24. 8. 14	Rouen	At Bruyeres Rest camp	
9 am	25. 8. 14	Rouen	Marched out of Bruyeres Rest camp. Entrained and left Rouen 3 pm. Arrived St Quentin 11.30 pm	
2.10 am.	26. 8. 14.	St Quentin	Detrained and proceeded to Rest Camp 1½ miles North of St Quentin. Reported to D.D.V.S. St Quentin 7 am and received orders to proceed with 4th Divisional units and report to A.D.V.S. of Division	
9 am.	do	do	Despatched two sick horses of 88th Battery R.F.A. to Base Vet: Hosp Amiens. Moved to Gare St Jeanne to await orders with other 4th Divisional units.	

2

WAR DIARY

or

~~INTELLIGENCE SUMMARY.~~

(Erase heading not required.)

Army Form C. 2118.

Instructions regarding War Diaries and Intelligence Summaries are contained in F. S. Regs., Part II. and the Staff Manual respectively. Title pages will be prepared in manuscript.

Hour, Date, Place	Summary of Events and Information	Remarks and references to Appendices
3.15 pm. 26. 8. 14. St Quentin	Marched to Ham where we arrived at 10 pm. Rained heavily on march and roads congested – Men wet through and standing in streets all night. No billets or stabling provided.	
5 am. 27. 8. 14 Ham	Continued march with 4th Divisional troops – Rained during march	
3 pm do Sempigny	Went into Camp	
28. 8. 14 do	D.D.V.S gave me orders to report to A.D.V.S. 4th Division when Division passes	
29. 8. 14 do	Despatched seven horses of 4th Divisional Units to Base Vety Hosp: Rouen.	
6 pm do do	Orders received from A.D.V.S. 4th Division to proceed to Compiegne and join 4th Divisional Ammunition Column and remain with them as a collecting station –	
10.20 pm do Compiegne	Arrived. No billets or stables for horses. Slept in street.	
30. 8. 14 do	Reported to Head Quarters. Saw D.D.V.S who gave me orders to send out men and try to find 4th Divisional Ammunition Column but almost immediately afterwards Major Conder A.D.V.S. 3rd Division saw me and said that D.D.V.S. had given him orders for me to join the 3rd Division and do duty under him – Orders from A.D.V.S. 3rd Division to march to La Vache Noire and report to Head Quarters there –	
8 am. 31. 8. 14. La Vache Noire	Marched with 3rd Division to Vauciennes and went into Camp at 6 pm.	

(9 26 6) W 257—976 100,000 4/12 H W V 79/3298

No 11. Mobile Vety: Section $\frac{121}{2165}$

Capt W R Meade [illegible]

—

Volume. II 1-30.9.14

(5 Sheets)

I

Instructions regarding War Diaries and Intelligence Summaries are contained in F. S. Regs., Part II. and the Staff Manual respectively. Title pages will be prepared in manuscript.

WAR DIARY
~~INTELLIGENCE~~ SUMMARY
(Erase heading not required.)

No XI Mobile Veterinary Section
W.R. Miele Capt AVC
O.C. XI M. V. S.

Army Form C. 2118.

Hour, Date, Place	Summary of Events and Information	Remarks and References to Appendices
10.15. a.m. 1. 9. 14 Vauciennes	Marched 10.15 a.m. for Villers St Genest where we arrived at 6.45 p.m and bivouaced.	
4. 30. a.m. 2. 9. 14. Villers-St-Genest.	Marched to Monthyon which we reached at 1 p.m. - Collected forty sick horses and marched at 3 p.m. to Meaux to endeavour to obtain trucks to evacuate the sick to Base - Obtained trucks at 10 p.m. and entrained the sick horses for Rouen. As there was no English officer on duty at station (R.T.O) considerable difficulty was experienced in making the station officials understand what was required as no interpreter had been allotted to my unit and it was essential that one should be available. Before leaving Monthyon for Meaux A. D. V. S. gave orders for the section to rejoin the Division at Lesches on the following day.	
8. 30. a.m. 3. 9. 14. Meaux	Marched for Lesches - Roads congested through movement of troops and impossible to march before - Arrived 11.30 a.m. and received orders from A. D. V. S. (through O.C. 3rd Div: Train) to take over eleven sick horses and rejoin Head Quarters, 3rd Div: at Pierre Levee - Found H^d Q^rs 3rd Div: at La Haute Maison where I reported & bivouaced at 7.45 p.m. - All along great difficulty experienced in drawing forage & rations as no second line transport available and the refilling point was some distance away - The forage cart as provided for transport of Vet^y Stores and section equipment absolutely inadequate and second line transport essential - Other units are provided with this.	

Instructions regarding War Diaries and Intelligence Summaries are contained in F. S. Regs., Part II. and the Staff Manual respectively. Title pages will be prepared in manuscript.

WAR DIARY ~~or~~ ~~INTELLIGENCE~~ SUMMARY.

(*Erase heading not required.*)

Army Form C. 2118.

2

Hour, Date, Place	Summary of Events and Information	Remarks and references to Appendices
12 noon. 4.9.14 La Haute-Maison	Under orders from A.D.V.S. marched with fourteen sick to Genevray there to collect sick from 3rd Div: Amm: Col: afterwards to proceed to Marles or nearest railhead to evacuate all sick to Lemans Collected nineteen sick from 3rd Div: Amm: Col: and continued march to Marles which was reached at 8.15 pm. Informed by R.T.O. no trucks available until morning. When the section is marching independently the want of a water cart is greatly felt, and even when marching with the Division other units will not allow us to use theirs.	
6.30 am. 5.9.14. Marles.	Informed by R.T.O. station closed so marched to Verneuil where there was a prospect of evacuating our sick. Arrived 1 pm. and had entrained sick horses by 6 pm. marched to rejoin Division at Le Mesnil (Chatres) where I arrived & reported to A.D.V.S. at 8 pm. Bivouaced. Still difficulty in obtaining supplies. The section is armed with a sword only and a firearm is necessary in view of the close proximity of the enemy. A revolver would appear to be the most useful weapon as it would serve the double purpose of defence and as a means of destroying horses incapable of or useless for further service which individuals of the sections are sent out to collect. A Humane Cattle Killer is not included in the equipment of a Mobile Veterinary Section.	

Instructions regarding War Diaries and Intelligence Summaries are contained in F. S. Regs., Part II. and the Staff Manual respectively. Title pages will be prepared in manuscript.

3

WAR DIARY

~~or~~

~~INTELLIGENCE SUMMARY.~~

(*Erase heading not required.*)

Army Form C. 2118.

Hour, Date, Place	Summary of Events and Information	Remarks and references to Appendices
6. 9. 14. Chatres	Collected 47 sick horses and marched to VERNEUIL - Entrained them for LEMANS and rejoined the Division at CREVECOEUR at which place the section bivouaced for night but the Division went on -	
6 am. 7. 9. 14 Crevecoeur	Marched for HAUTFEUILLE and rejoined Division - Collected 56 sick horses - Received orders from A.D.V.S. to march back early in the morning and evacuate our sick -	
6 am. 8. 9. 14 Hautfeuille	Marched with 53 sick horses, handed over one more and entrained 54 at VERNEUIL - Marched back as far as MARLES and bivouaced for night. The personnel of the section is too small to permit efficiency, it being necessary for each man to lead four and sometimes five or six horses apiece, local labour not being available. This hampers mobility [illegible] blocks the roads and exhausts the sick horses -	
6.30 am. 9. 9. 14. Marles	Marched to ~~[illegible]~~ rejoin the division - On arrival at a point 2.8 Kil: south of Saacy found the Artillery in action so could not proceed. Stood fast until 7.30 pm when we went into bivouac -	
5.0 am 10. 9. 14. Saacy.	Marched & rejoined Division at BEZU-LE-GUICY - After a short halt continued march with the Division to CHEZY-EN-OROXOIS. Raining -	
6 am. 11. 9. 14 Chezy-en-Oroxois.	Marched with Division to GRAND ROZOY - Arrived 7 pm Rained very heavily -	
8.30 am. 12. 9. 14 Grand Rozoy	Marched for Presles - Heavy action going on and many halts - Eventually reached CERCEUIL at 9.30 pm - Village blocked with troops and impossible to get billets - It had rained very heavily all afternoon and evening & men were wet through - Had to stand in rain all night it being impossible to bivouac - Horses were left standing in harness -	

(9 26 6) W 257—976 100,000 4/12 H W V 79/3298

4

WAR DIARY

~~or~~

~~INTELLIGENCE~~ SUMMARY.

(*Erase heading not required.*)

Army Form C. 2118.

Instructions regarding War Diaries and Intelligence Summaries are contained in F. S. Regs., Part II. and the Staff Manual respectively. Title pages will be prepared in manuscript.

Hour, Date, Place	Summary of Events and Information	Remarks and references to Appendices
8.30 am 13.9.14 Cerseuil	Marched into BRAINE and billeted. Heavy action all day.	
14.9.14 Braine	Did not move during morning owing to battle proceeding. At 2 pm A.D.V.S. arrived with Remounts. Received orders to go back to CUIRY HOUSSE collecting sick on the way also look after some Remounts he had left at CUIRY HOUSSE footsore, shoe the latter and make CUIRY HOUSSE my Head Quarters for the time being.	
15.9.14 Cuiry Housse	Remained at CUIRY HOUSSE. Found that all remounts left behind required shoeing but no shoeing smith is included in the Section War Establishment. Fortunately my groom and Senior N.C.O. were previously shoeing smiths and they carried out the shoeing of these horses. One or two shoeing smiths are essential in the Section. Collected more sick.	
16.9.14 ditto	Marched into FERE-EN-TARDENOIS with a detachment and sixty sick horses. Head Quarters of Section remained at CUIRY HOUSSE and shoeing of Remounts proceeded with. Detachment sent out to try and pick up Remounts left behind by A.D.V.S. on his march from railhead to the Division. Reported to D.D.V.S. at FERE-EN-TARDENOIS and received orders not to send any more sick to LEMANS but remain in camp for the present.	
17.9.14 Fere-en-Tardenois	Received orders from D.D.V.S. to hand over my sick horses to O.C. No 1 Mobile Vety Section, send to CUIRY HOUSSE for the remainder of my Section and proceed to VICHEL-NANTEVIL to take over thirteen Remounts (and shoe them) which were there in charge of the Mayor. Marched at 12 noon and arrived at 6 pm. Very wet.	

(9 26 6) W 257—976 100,000 4/12 H W V 79/3298

5

Instructions regarding War Diaries and Intelligence Summaries are contained in F. S. Regs., Part II. and the Staff Manual respectively. Title pages will be prepared in manuscript.

WAR DIARY
~~or~~
~~INTELLIGENCE~~ SUMMARY
(Erase heading not required.)

Army Form C. 2118.

Hour, Date, Place	Summary of Events and Information	Remarks and References to Appendices
18-9-14. Vichel-Nanteuil	Remained in VICHEL all day shoeing Remounts - orders from D.D.V.S. to make Pte Keen, one of my batmen a shoeing smith.	
5.30 am. 19.9.14 ditto	Found three of the thirteen Remounts unfit to proceed - Marched with the remaining ten to FERE-EN-TARDENOIS. Where I received orders from D.D.V.S. to proceed to CUIRY HOUSSE, pick up the Remounts which I had had shod and left there and then rejoin the Division - Arrived CUIRY HOUSSE 5 pm and billeted -	
20.9.14 - Cuiry Housse	Marched into BRAINE with Remounts and handed them over to A.D.V.S. - Collected sick from various units of the Division and turned them into a paddock for the night - Returned to CUIRY HOUSSE where Head Quarters of Section had remained and found more sick had been handed in - Rained heavily during day -	
21.9.14 ditto	Marched into BRAINE with sick - Collected those left in paddock previous night and entrained a total of sixty four to Base Vety: Hosp: Billeted in BRAINE.	
22 to 30-9.14 Braine	Collecting sick daily and entraining them to Base Vet?: Hosp: as opportunity arose - over two hundred sick animals were evacuated during this period - Also a second cart and harness requisitioned -	

No 11. Mobile Veterinary Section

Vol: II

121
1363

W.D.

Oct 1914
Sept

Army Form C. 2118.

Instructions regarding War Diaries and Intelligence Summaries are contained in F. S. Regs., Part II. and the Staff Manual respectively. Title pages will be prepared in manuscript.

WAR DIARY
or
INTELLIGENCE SUMMARY
(Erase heading not required.)

Hour, Date, Place	Summary of Events and Information	Remarks and References to Appendices
1. 9. 14 VILLIERS. St GENESTE.	Captain Gibbs and Lieut LITTLE rejoined, the former missed his way, the latter dislocated his shoulder & has been in hospital at St QUENTIN, he is now fit for duty but cannot ride. No 11. M.V.S took over several sick. I proceeded by motor car to PLESSIS DE BELLEVILLE & endeavour to get a train for sick horses, arrived to find the ~~Staff leaving~~ Railway Staff leaving, Germans being reported within 4 miles.	
2. 9. 4 MONTHYON	Marched 6 a.m. arrived in camp at 1 pm. No 11 M.V.S left at 3.30 pm. with 40 sick which are to be evacuated at MEAUX. ~~Station~~ Captain Neale has orders to proceed to LEECHES and await orders. I have to day been informed that Lieut FOX A.V.C was killed at AUDENCOURT & was seen dead by a sergeant of the R.I. Regt. Unable to verify this	
3. 9. 4 LA HAUTE MAISON	Proceeded by car to Leeches with orders for the Div Train, Field Ambulances and M.V.S to proceed to LA HAUTE MAISON. No 11. M.V.S not at LEECHES but it arrived in camp at 7 pm having evacuated sick at MEAUX.	

(9 26 6) W 257—976 100,000 4/12 H W V 79/3298

Instructions regarding War Diaries and Intelligence Summaries are contained in F. S. Regs., Part II. and the Staff Manual respectively. Title pages will be prepared in manuscript.

WAR DIARY
or
INTELLIGENCE SUMMARY
(Erase heading not required.)

Army Form C. 2118.

Hour, Date, Place	Summary of Events and Information	Remarks and References to Appendices
4. 9.14 LA HAUTE MAISON	No 11 M.V.S. left at NOON with 14 sick is to pick up 19 from Ammunition Column at GENEVY. and then proceed to railhead evacuate sick and return to the division. There is always considerable difficulty in obtaining rations for the M.V.S as Supply Officers state they are L. of C units. Interviewed D.A.Q.M.G. he has ordered that rations for them shall be drawn with H.Q 3rd Division. Marched at 1 pm halted at 2 pm until 6 pm when we proceeded to Le GRAND CORT which place we left at midnight	
5. 9. 14 CHATRES	Arrived at 8 a.m. after a tiring night march Visited Royal Irish Regt. + interviewed Sergt EAGER N.C.O i/c transport, who stated that "He knew Lieut FOX well + he saw him at Chapel at AUDENCOURT He was dead" - Officially reported Lt FOX as "Killed" No 11. M.V.S having evacuated sick at VERNEUILL arrived at CHATRES at 8 p.m -	

Army Form C. 2118.

Instructions regarding War Diaries and Intelligence Summaries are contained in F. S. Regs., Part II. and the Staff Manual respectively. Title pages will be prepared in manuscript.

WAR DIARY
or
INTELLIGENCE SUMMARY
(Erase heading not required.)

Hour, Date, Place	Summary of Events and Information	Remarks and References to Appendices
6. 9. 14. CHATRES	Purchased horse, cart and harness for use as an office for G.O.C 3rd Division. Cost fr. 1550 — No 11. M.V.S with 47 sick left for railhead. Marched at 8 Am. Arrived HAUTEFEUILLE at 7.3.0 pm.	
7. 9. 14. HAUTEFEUILLE	Visited 9 Inf Bde. 23 + 42 Bde R.F.A. and arranged for sick to be collected at HAUTEFEUILLE. NEALE with 11. M.V.S arrived at 9 Am having evacuated sick. Handed over 56 sick to him & ordered him to proceed to railhead at day break tomorrow. He has orders to return to H.Q. 3rd Division when sick have been disposed of. Marched at 1 pm arrived at ~~[illegible]~~ BOISSY LE CHATEAU at 6 pm.	
8. 9. 14. BUSSIERES	Marched at 5 Am. Fighting took place during greater part of the day. Arrived at BUSSIERES at 5 p.m. —	

Army Form C. 2118.

Instructions regarding War Diaries and Intelligence Summaries are contained in F. S. Regs., Part II. and the Staff Manual respectively. Title pages will be prepared in manuscript.

WAR DIARY
or
INTELLIGENCE SUMMARY
(Erase heading not required.)

Hour, Date, Place	Summary of Events and Information	Remarks and References to Appendices
9.9.14. BEZU LE GUERY	Marched at 5 am. Fighting took place greater part of the day. I have been ordered to attend to all matters relating to remounts. Arrived at Bezu le Guery at 10 pm.	
10.9.14 COULOMMIERS	Proceeded at day break to COULOMMIERS to take over remounts for the division, these 307 in number were detrained at 5 pm. Many are unshod whilst nearly all require shoeing. Placed them in a paddock for the night. Ordered Captain Leckie No. 7 M.V.S to proceed to BEZU LE GUERY to collect sick there & to march to railhead when he had collected 20 or more sick. Inform Col Butler that No. 7 & 11 M.V.S were now with 3rd Division – I did not require both. He ordered me to send Capt Leckie with No. 7 M.V.S to the Cavalry Division. Met Captain Neale with No. 11 M.V.S about 1½ miles from Bezu le Guery ordered him to proceed in rear of division collecting any sick left behind & to camp in villages nearest in rear of Hd Qrs of 3rd Division.	

Instructions regarding War Diaries and Intelligence Summaries are contained in F. S. Regs., Part II. and the Staff Manual respectively. Title pages will be prepared in manuscript.

WAR DIARY
or
INTELLIGENCE SUMMARY
(Erase heading not required.)

Army Form C. 2118.

Hour, Date, Place	Summary of Events and Information	Remarks and References to Appendices
11. 9 14. MONTREUIL	Marched at 5 30 am from COULOMMIERS with 307 remounts & 81 men. Arrived at 3 30 pm. at Montreuil where we remained for the night. Horses placed in paddocks. Hay & oat hay placed about paddock. Many horses are already lame owing to want of shoes. Left one horse, badly kicked on forearm at DEBOMMET farm, one died suddenly on road. Experienced great difficulty in getting horses along. Halters constantly break & nearly all men have 4 horses. Raining heavily since 12 noon.	
12. 9 14 VICHEL	Marched at 8 am having previously watered & fed horses on oat hay. Left 4 horses which too lame to march. Halted at noon for 3 hours at CHEZY where horses were watered & turned into a lucerne field to graze. 5 had to be left here unable to march owing to sore feet due to being unshod. Arrived at Vichel at 6 30 pm	

Instructions regarding War Diaries and Intelligence Summaries are contained in F. S. Regs., Part II. and the Staff Manual respectively. Title pages will be prepared in manuscript.

WAR DIARY
or
INTELLIGENCE SUMMARY
(Erase heading not required.)

Army Form C. 2118.

Hour, Date, Place	Summary of Events and Information	Remarks and References to Appendices
12.9.14 (continued)	Horses placed in paddock + hay strewn about the place. About 20 horses lost in a stampede caused by motor lorries. Several others probably about 15 left on road unable to proceed. Have had great trouble with the men there are only 2 bombardiers with these men + they have little or no control over them. Heavy rain during greater part of day + night.	
~~13.9.14~~ 13.9.14. CURY HOUSSE	Marched at 8 AM. Halted 11 AM near HARTENNES. Left 8 horses at VICHEL and 5 others at midday halt where horses were watered + turned into a clover field to graze. I counted horses here total 228. Proceeded at 1.30 pm. Met Divisional Ammunition Column at 4 pm near CURY HOUSSE, obtained 1 Sgt + six men with saddles to assist. Horses placed in ~~f~~ stables at CURY HOUSSE. Men have no rations. Requisitioned 2 sheep + flour for men + ample hay for horses.	

(9 26 6) W 257—976 100,000 4/12 H W V 79/3298

Instructions regarding War Diaries and Intelligence Summaries are contained in F. S. Regs., Part II. and the Staff Manual respectively. Title pages will be prepared in manuscript.

WAR DIARY
or
INTELLIGENCE SUMMARY
(Erase heading not required.)

Army Form C. 2118.

Hour, Date, Place	Summary of Events and Information	Remarks and References to Appendices
14 9 14 CURY HOUSSE	Marched at 8 AM. 12 horses left behind unfit to march all lame in feet due to ~~want~~ not being shod. Came up with Divisional Train about 1½ miles from here. Col. Rycroft, II Corps & Lt Col. Longmore saw horses the former ordered me to hand over all unshod horses to Divisional Train and Ammunition Column. Carried horses numbering 195. Handed 30 to Divisional Train 39 to Ammunition Column and 26 to No 11 M.V.S the latter 26 are lame & have badly broken feet.	
14.9.14 BRAINE	Reported to Hd Qrs that I had 105 remounts fit for issue. Units at present heavily engaged. Turned horses into a large field where there is good grazing & water, also strewed hay about the field. Saw Col. Butler who took a statement from me regarding remounts.	

(9 26 6) W 257—976 100,000 4/12 H W V 79/3298

Instructions regarding War Diaries and Intelligence Summaries are contained in F. S. Regs., Part II. and the Staff Manual respectively. Title pages will be prepared in manuscript.

WAR DIARY
or
INTELLIGENCE SUMMARY.
(Erase heading not required.)

Army Form C. 2118.

Hour, Date, Place	Summary of Events and Information	Remarks and references to Appendices
14. 9. 14. Braine	Neale with No 11. M.V.S. reported about noon. Ordered him to proceed to CURY HOUSSE after taking over sick from Divisional Train and Ammunition Column. To send a party back to HARTENNES to search for [illegible] left by me. Total sick at CURY HOUSSE is 60 of these 38 are remounts latter are to be shod as early as possible.	
15. 9. 14 Braine	14 sick sent to No 11. M.V.S at CURY HOUSSE. Some remounts handed over to Field Ambulance. Am arranging to issue heavy draught horses for the ambulances as I consider the waggon is too heavy for a pair of light draught horses.	
16. 9. 14. BRAINE	Remainder of remounts handed over to RA + RE. No 11 MVS with 60 sick proceeded to Fère en Tardenois. Sgt Mason and Pte Reece remained at Cury House ~~to~~ they are shoeing the remounts. I visited Cury House at 3 pm 24 remounts are there	

Army Form C. 2118.

Instructions regarding War Diaries and Intelligence Summaries are contained in F. S. Regs., Part II. and the Staff Manual respectively. Title pages will be prepared in manuscript.

WAR DIARY
or
~~INTELLIGENCE SUMMARY.~~
(Erase heading not required.)

Hour, Date, Place	Summary of Events and Information	Remarks and references to Appendices
17. 9. 14. BRAINE	Visited Cury Housse. Sgt MARSON + Pte KEENE have rejoined section which is now at FERE EN TARDENOIS. Cpl. HARDWICKE + two men returned to Cury Housse they had been unable to trace any remounts stolen here and HARTENNES. Several remounts now sound.	
18. 9. 14. BRAINE	Visited CURY HOUSSE and sent 8 of the 24 remounts to BRAINE to join division, they are sound + fit for work. NEALE with No 11 M.V.S. still away	
19. 9. 14 BRAINE	Visited RE at CHASSEMY. several horses have been killed + wounded during the last few days, otherwise horses are doing well, galls healing + horses are picking up in condition. Ordered L^c SNEYD to take charge of them	
	Visited Cury HOUSSE + met NEALE with No 11 M.V.S marching in. He reports having found 13 horses at VICHEL, 10 of these he shod + has brought with him the remaining 3 were too lame to move and have been left in charge of the mayor. I took one remount back to H Q 3rd Division	

(9 26 6) W 257—976 100,000 4/12 H W V 79/3298

Instructions regarding War Diaries and Intelligence Summaries are contained in F. S. Regs., Part II. and the Staff Manual respectively. Title pages will be prepared in manuscript.

WAR DIARY
or
~~INTELLIGENCE SUMMARY.~~
(Erase heading not required.)

Army Form C. 2118

Hour, Date, Place	Summary of Events and Information	Remarks and references to Appendices
20. 9. 14 BRAINE	Captain NEALE arrived with 19 remounts fit for issue + took over 43 sick these were placed in a field for the night They will probably be entrained here tomorrow He returned to CURY HOUSSE where No 11 M.V.S still is and also 6 remounts. 13 sick from Ammunition Column sent to CURY HOUSSE Horses have been on short rations of oats for several days I spoke to D.A.Q.M.G. about this	
21. 9. 14 BRAINE	64 sick horses entrained by No 11 M.V.S which arrived here at 11 A.m. Men billeted in a barn, close to a suitable field for sick horses. 31 sick received + turned loose into field for night Hope to entrain them tomorrow Difficulty experienced in obtaining rations for No 11 M.V.S as they have no cart to go to refilling point 2 remounts had been left at CURY HOUSSE until evening when one was destroyed + the other shod + brought to BRAINE	

(9 26 6) W 257—976 100,000 4/12 H W V 79/3298

Army Form C. 2118.

Instructions regarding War Diaries and Intelligence Summaries are contained in F. S. Regs., Part II. and the Staff Manual respectively. Title pages will be prepared in manuscript.

WAR DIARY
or
~~INTELLIGENCE SUMMARY.~~
(Erase heading not required.)

Hour, Date, Place	Summary of Events and Information	Remarks and references to Appendices
22. 9. 14. BRAINE	273. Remounts arrived at 7.30 am - detrained and issued to units. Horses are in good condition and of a suitable class.	
	30 sick horses entrained by No 11. M.V.S.	
23. 9. 14. BRAINE	Obtained sanction from A A Q M G (Col BOYLE) to requisition a cart & harness for mobile section as great difficulty is experienced in getting rations because they have no cart to send to the refilling point. Obtained a suitable cart and harness for francs (Three hundred) & gave a requisition paper. I could not pay for these because the owner was away and the Mayor of Braine refused to take cash. The Mayor sent a man with me to value cart & harness.	
	There is considerable difficulty experienced in getting the Field Ambulances horses shod - a shoeing smith should be posted to these units. G.O.C has sent in an application to 2nd Army Corps.	

(9 26 6) W 257—976 100,000 4/12 H W V 70/3298

Army Form C. 2118.

Instructions regarding War Diaries and Intelligence Summaries are contained in F. S. Regs., Part II. and the Staff Manual respectively. Title pages will be prepared in manuscript.

WAR DIARY
or
~~INTELLIGENCE SUMMARY.~~
(Erase heading not required.)

Hour, Date, Place	Summary of Events and Information	Remarks and references to Appendices
24. 9. 14. BRAINE	Visited 42nd Bde. Ammunition Column 40th Bde R.F.A. and 44 Bde R.G.A. Horses are improving daily. Col. Butler arrived about 4.30 pm. & said the horses of the Bridging Train R.E. were looking very bad & not receiving proper attention, that they should be making great improvement as they are living in a "Land of Plenty". I explained that the horses of the division were not receiving a full ration of oats & that I had informed Supply Officer that it was most necessary horses should receive full rations. ~~Capt~~ I placed Captain Anderson A.V.C. in charge of this unit which has only recently joined this division. Inspected them myself. 49 sick entrained for Villeneuve St Georges.	
25. 9. 14 BRAINE	Inspected Bridging Train and Field Ambulance No 9. Field Ambulance has only received [illegible] lbs oats a day. Col. Butler called & personally interviewed Maj DAVIS D.A.Q.M.G re horse rations. No 103 Siege Battery with Lt SELBART A.V.C. arrived	

(9 26 6) W 257—976 100,000 4/12 H W V 79/3298

Instructions regarding War Diaries and Intelligence Summaries are contained in F. S. Regs., Part II. and the Staff Manual respectively. Title pages will be prepared in manuscript.

WAR DIARY
or
INTELLIGENCE SUMMARY.
(Erase heading not required.)

Army Form C. 2118

Hour, Date, Place	Summary of Events and Information	Remarks and references to Appendices
26.9.14 BRAINE	Col. Butler arrived about 11 a.m. I accompanied him around following units Bridging Train, Divisional Train and Ammunition Column, 7th Bde Infantry Transport 40th Bde R.F.A. 8th Field Ambulance. 40th Bde horses had no hay they returned yesterday at 7 a.m. from an artillery position. Col. Butler interviewed Col. Elkington O.C. 40 Bde and Major Farmar D.A.Q.M.G. on subject of horse rations. 51. sick evacuated by No. 11 M.V.S to Villeneuve.	
27.9.14. BRAINE.	Proceeded to CHASSEMY inspected horses of 56. Co. R.E and Compo Co. R.E. These horses are placed in a wood, where it is necessary to keep them as they are at once shelled unless they are carefully concealed. 3 were killed shortly after I left. They are in rather poor condition I ~~[illegible]~~ ordered 4 to be sent to the mobile section all cases of debility.	
28.9.10. BRAINE	Visited No. 9 Field Ambulance at COURCELLES condition of horses is good but several are in want of shoeing, arranged for a farrier to be sent from No. 29 Co. A.S.C. A shoeing smith should be appointed to each Field Ambulance. 42nd Bde R.F.A arrived at BRAINE from BRENELLE artillery position for 3 days rest. Horses are in good condition	

Instructions regarding War Diaries and Intelligence Summaries are contained in F. S. Regs., Part II. and the Staff Manual respectively. Title pages will be prepared in manuscript.

WAR DIARY
or
INTELLIGENCE SUMMARY.
(Erase heading not required.)

Army Form C. 2118.

Hour, Date, Place	Summary of Events and Information	Remarks and references to Appendices
29. 9. 14. BRAINE	Lt Jelbart ordered to proceed to Mont Notre Dame Headquarters of Siege Artillery, placed Captain Gibbs i/c Siege battery. 4 suspicious cases of Epizootic lymphangitis among horses of the Bridging Train. Held a consultation with Captains Neale, Gibbs + Anderson. We are all agreed that the cases are most suspicious. Reported by wire to D.D.V.S and sent Pte MOORE No. 11. M.V.S to Villeneuve St George with pus for microscopical examination. Unable to procure a microscope here. Destroyed one of the above suspects.	
30. 9. 14. BRAINE	Col. Butler. D.D.V.S arrived + inspected ~~[illegible]~~ suspected cases of Epizootic lymphangitis. He considered I had not acted wisely. I should have obtained a car + seen him personally before taking any steps. My action in sending pus for microscopical examination was not justified without first consulting him. I had ~~just~~ destroyed one case just before he arrived. He interviewed Col. Boyle A A Q M G on subject	

(9 26 6) W 257—976 100,000 4/12 H W V 79/3298

121/1967

11. Mobile Vety: Sections.

Vol III. 1–31.10.14

A.V.D

Capt Neale

1

W R Meale / Capt AVC
OC XI Mob. Vety Sectn Army Form C. 2118.

Instructions regarding War Diaries and Intelligence Summaries are contained in F. S. Regs., Part II. and the Staff Manual respectively. Title pages will be prepared in manuscript.

WAR DIARY
or
~~INTELLIGENCE SUMMARY~~

(Erase heading not required.)

Hour, Date, Place	Summary of Events and Information	Remarks and References to Appendices
1st + 2nd 10.14. BRAINE	Collecting sick horses	
7.30 am. 3-10-14 ditto	Marched to MONT NOTRE DAME and entrained 47 sick for Base. On completion of this continued march to ARCY-STE-RESTITUTE and rejoined H.Qrs 3rd Division at 1-10 pm	
6 pm do ARCY	Marched with Division to LA FERTE MILON and arrived there 3.30 am. 4/10/14 -	
5.30 pm. 4-10-14 LA FERTE MILON	Marched with Division and arrived at CREPY EN VALOIS about midnight	
9-30 am. 5-10-14 CREPY-EN-VALOIS	Marched with Division to PONT-ST-MAXENCE arriving there about 4-15 pm. In rest camp until 10.30 pm at which hour entrained -	
9-30 am. 6-10-14 ABBEVILLE	Arrived - Received orders to detrain at 12 noon and bivouaced on canal bank for the night.	
9 am. 7-10-14 ditto	Moved with section into Cavalry barracks - Later received orders to move into billet 2 miles North of the town -	
8-10-14 ditto	Collecting sick also received a batch of Remounts and afterwards assisted in issuing them.	
9-10-14 ditto	Under orders from A.D.V.S. 3rd Division handed over 55 sick horses to the French authorities at Cavalry barracks, ABBEVILLE - Marched at 3 pm and arrived LABROYE at 6.15 pm and bivouaced.	
8.30 am. 10-10-14 LABROYE	Marched for PERNES - Received orders en route to collect 3 sick horses at REGNAUVILLE and evacuate them at HESDIN. Did so and continued march to PERNES where arrived at 8 pm.	

(9 26 6) W 257—976 100,000 4/12 H W V 79/3298

Instructions regarding War Diaries and Intelligence Summaries are contained in F. S. Regs., Part II. and the Staff Manual respectively. Title pages will be prepared in manuscript.

2

WAR DIARY

~~or~~

INTELLIGENCE ~~SUMMARY~~

(*Erase heading not required.*)

Army Form C. 2118.

Hour, Date, Place	Summary of Events and Information	Remarks and References to Appendices
11. 10. 14. PERNES	Collecting sick.	
12. 10. 14 ditto	Marched to WAVRAN and entrained 18 sick. Returned & bivouaced.	
8.30 am 13. 10. 14 ditto	Marched to rejoin the Division and reported to A.D.V.S. at 4.30 pm at ZELOBES. Received orders to billet there.	
14–16. 10. 14 ZELOBES	Collecting sick	
9 am 17. 10. 14 ditto	Marched with sick for PERNES. Orders to collect 3 sick horses on the way which had been left at different villages. Arrived PERNES 4.30 pm. Informed by R.T.O. it was still railhead but doubtful if it would be so tomorrow.	
18. 10. 14 PERNES	Railhead changed to BETHUNE. No possibility of obtaining trucks at PERNES	
12.15 pm do do →	Marched for BETHUNE. Arrived 4.15 pm and entrained the sick. Both the R.T.O. and O/c of the train informed me they would not take sick horses unless some men accompanied them to their destination. Fortunately No 5 M.V.S. were also evacuating sick and had 5 men going down so I was able to entrain my 28. Returned to ZELOBES.	
19. 10. 14 ZELOBES	Under orders from A.D.V.S. proceeded to PONT LOGY and billeted Collecting sick	
8 am 20. 10. 14 PONT LOGY	Proceeded to BETHUNE station and took over a batch of Remounts returning with them to PONT LOGY where they were issued by ADVS. to units. Collecting sick	

Instructions regarding War Diaries and Intelligence Summaries are contained in F. S. Regs., Part II. and the Staff Manual respectively. Title pages will be prepared in manuscript.

WAR DIARY

~~or~~

~~INTELLIGENCE~~ SUMMARY

(*Erase heading not required.*)

Army Form C. 2118.

Hour, Date, Place	Summary of Events and Information	Remarks and References to Appendices
21. 10. 14 PONT LOGY	Received orders to move section to VIEILLE CHAPELLE. Marched there and arrived at noon. Collecting sick.	
22. 10. 14 VIEILLE CHAPELLE	– Collecting sick	
11.45am 23.10.14 ditto	Marched to LILLERS and evacuated 43 sick horses. Returned to VIEILLE CHAPELLE.	
24.10.14 ditto	Collecting sick	
25-10-14 ditto	ditto	
26-10-14 ditto	ditto	
12.30pm 27-10.14 ditto	Marched with sick on the way to railhead and billeted for night at LAPUGNOY	
11am 28-10.14 LAPUGNOY	– Marched for railhead at PERNES and entrained 44 sick. Returned to LAPUGNOY and billeted for the night.	
9am 29.10.14 ditto	Marched for VIEILLE CHAPELLE and arrived at noon. Received orders to move to LESTREM and billet there	
30+31-10-14 LESTREM.	Collecting sick	

V D

L. of C.

121
2599

No 11. Mobile Veterinary Section.

Vol IV.

1.

W. R. Meale | Captain A.V.C.
O.C. No. XI Mobile Veterinary Section

Army Form C. 2118.

WAR DIARY
or
~~INTELLIGENCE SUMMARY.~~
(*Erase heading not required.*)

Instructions regarding War Diaries and Intelligence Summaries are contained in F.S. Regs., Part II. and the Staff Manual respectively. Title pages will be prepared in manuscript.

Hour, Date, Place	Summary of Events and Information	Remarks and references to Appendices
LESTREM. 1-11-14	Collecting sick	
11. am. do 2. 11. 14	Marched to STRAZEELE with 32 sick and evacuated them to Base Veterinary Hospital – Took over 20 Remounts out of a batch which had been sent up for the Division and returned to billet at LESTREM	
do 3.11.14	Disposed of Remounts to units – Proceeded to GONNEHEM to collect sick horses which had been left behind by units on the march – Admitting sick	
do 4.11.14	Collecting sick	
do 5.11.14	ditto	
do 6.11.14	Marched to STRAZEELE with 43 sick and entrained ~~for~~ them for the base – Head Quarters left at LESTREM and collected 25 sick during my absence at railhead. Received orders from A.D.V.S. to proceed to MOOLENACKER in the morning and billet there.	
do 7.11.14	Marched with 25 sick and entrained them at STRAZEELE continued march to MOOLENACKER and billeted –	
MOOLENACKER. 8.11.14	Received orders from A.D.V.S. to return to LESTREM in the morning as it would be a more convenient point for collecting sick from units of the 3rd Division	

(73989) W4141—463. 400,000. 9/14. H.&J.Ltd. Forms/C. 2118/10.

2

Army Form C. 2118.

Instructions regarding War Diaries and Intelligence Summaries are contained in F. S. Regs., Part II. and the Staff Manual respectively. Title pages will be prepared in manuscript.

WAR DIARY
~~or~~
~~INTELLIGENCE SUMMARY.~~

(Erase heading not required.)

Hour, Date, Place	Summary of Events and Information	Remarks and references to Appendices
10 am. MOOLENACKER. 9/11/14	Marched for LESTREM via BAILLEUL and STEENWERCK. Collected 6 horses at the latter place and arrived LESTREM 3.30pm. Billeted.	
LESTREM. 10.11.14	Collecting sick	
ditto 11.11.14	Marched to HAZEBROUCK and entrained 36 sick. Returned to LESTREM. Orders received from A.D.V.S. that the section was to be armed with pistols & rifles and swords to be handed in to the A.O.D.	
ditto 12 to 14.11.14	Collecting sick	
1 pm. ditto 15.11.14	Marched to MERVILLE and entrained 42 sick. Billeted in the town.	
9 am. MERVILLE. 16.11.14	Marched to METEREN and billeted.	
METEREN. 17.11.14	Collecting sick. Orders received that in future conducting parties from personnel of section were to accompany sick horses evacuated to Base.	
ditto 18.11.14	Collecting sick.	

3

Instructions regarding War Diaries and Intelligence Summaries are contained in F. S. Regs., Part II. and the Staff Manual respectively. Title pages will be prepared in manuscript.

WAR DIARY

or

~~INTELLIGENCE~~ SUMMARY.

(*Erase heading not required.*)

Army Form C. 2118.

Hour, Date, Place	Summary of Events and Information	Remarks and references to Appendices
METEREN. 19.11.14.	Received orders from A.D.V.S. to proceed to BOESCHEPE and billet there, but on arrival found it impossible as every available space was occupied by French troops. Found there was accomodation at BERTHEN about 2 miles South so billeted there. Very severe snow storm.	
BERTHEN. 20.11.14.	Marched to BAILLEUL and entrained 16 sick to base. 7 men and 4 horses joined section on increase of establishment. Returned to billet at BERTHEN.	
ditto 21 to 25.11.14	At BERTHEN. Collecting sick	
ditto 26.11.14.	Collecting sick. 4 men joined the section on increase of establishment.	
ditto 27.11.14.	Marched to BAILLEUL and entrained 12 sick for base. Returned to BERTHEN.	
ditto 28/11/14 to 30/11/14	Collecting sick	

(73989) W4141—463. 400,000. 9/14. H.&J.Ltd. Forms/C. 2118/10.

A.V.D

3rd Division

121 / 3944

No 11. Mobile. Vety: Sect.

Vol V. 1 – 31.12.14

1

W R Neale / Capt AVC
O.C. No XI Mob: Vet: Sect

Army Form C. 2118

Instructions regarding War Diaries and Intelligence Summaries are contained in F. S. Regs., Part II. and the Staff Manual respectively. Title pages will be prepared in manuscript.

11 MOBILE VETERINARY SECTION

WAR DIARY
or
~~INTELLIGENCE SUMMARY.~~

(Erase heading not required.)

Hour, Date, Place	Summary of Events and Information	Remarks and references to Appendices
1. 12. 14 BERTHEN	Collecting Sick – One shoeing smith joined the section on increase of establishment. Handed over command to Lt Sewell prior to proceeding on six day leave	
2/12/14 Berthen	Assumed command of No. XI Mobile Veterinary Section during the absence on leave of Capt. Neale. Collected sick	E. Sewell Lt. AVC (SR)
3/12/14 Berthen. 1Pg.	Marched to Bailleul & entrained 15 sick horses for advanced Veterinary Hospital. Returned to billet at Berthen on completion of this duty	E.S.
(4/12/14 – 7/12/14) Berthen	Remained at Berthen collecting sick. very wet	E.S.
8. 12. 14 BERTHEN	Resumed command of section – Collecting sick	
9. 12. 14 ditto	Marched to BAILLEUL and entrained twenty sick horses for Base and returned to billet.	
10th to 13th 12. 14 ditto	Collecting sick	
14. 12. 14 ditto	Marched to BAILLEUL and entrained nine sick horses for base. Also sent scrapings down from two suspected mange cases for microscopical exam: – Returned to billet	

(9 26 6) W 257—976 100,000 4/12 H W V $\frac{79}{3298}$

2

Army Form C. 21[illegible]

Instructions regarding War Diaries and Intelligence Summaries are contained in F. S. Regs., Part II. and the Staff Manual respectively. Title pages will be prepared in manuscript.

WAR DIARY ~~or~~ INTELLIGENCE ~~SUMMARY~~.

(Erase heading not required.)

Hour, Date, Place	Summary of Events and Information	Remarks and references to Appendices
15th + 16th. 12. 14. BERTHEN	Collecting sick	
17. 12. 14 ditto	Marched to BAILLEUL and entrained twenty one sick horses for Base. Fourteen cases sent to BOULOGNE and seven suspected Mange Cases to ABBEVILLE.	
18th to 20th 12. 14 ditto	Collecting sick –	
21 - 12. 14 ditto	Marched to BAILLEUL and entrained thirty five sick horses for the Base – Returned to billet –	
22nd to 25th 12. 14 ditto	Collecting sick	
26. 12. 14 ditto	Marched to ~~Bea~~ BAILLEUL and entrained eighteen sick horses to BOULOGNE and six suspected mange cases to ABBEVILLE – Returned to billet – One Shoeing Smith posted to No. X Vet: Hosp: for permanent duty –	
27th to 31st 12. 14 ditto	Collecting sick –	

Index

SUBJECT.

No.	Contents.	Date.
	3RD DIV,	
	11TH MOBILE VET'Y SECTION.	
	WAR DIARY,	
	JAN - DEC, 1915	

(56,425). Wt.24,741—161. 2000. 11/20. Gp.164. A.&E.W.

AVD

3rd Division

121
4327

11th Mobile Vety. Section.

Vol VI.

Jan 1915

Instructions regarding War Diaries and Intelligence Summaries are contained in F. S. Regs., Part II. and the Staff Manual respectively. Title pages will be prepared in manuscript.

1 I

WAR DIARY
or
~~INTELLIGENCE SUMMARY~~.
(Erase heading not required.)

W. W. Rheale / Capt. AVC
O.C. XI Mobile Vet. Sect.

Army Form C. 2118.

Hour, Date, Place	Summary of Events and Information	Remarks and references to Appendices
Jany 1st & 2nd 1915. BERTHEN.	Collecting sick. Wet ground & roads in very bad condition	
" 3rd " "	Collecting sick. Staff Sergt. McSherry left the section to join No. X Vet. Hospital on promotion.	
" 4th " "	Collecting sick.	
" 5th " "	Marched to STEENWERCK, as BAILLEUL station temporarily closed for movement of troops, and entrained 25 sick horses for NEUFCHATEL. PAS DE CALAIS	
" 6th " "	Marched to BAILLEUL and entrained 19 suspected mange cases for ABBEVILLE	
" 7th to 11th " "	~~At~~ Collecting sick. DDVS. visited the section on 9th inst	
" 12th " "	Marched to BAILLEUL and entrained 18 sick horses for NEUFCHATEL.	
" 13th & 14th "	Collecting sick. DDVS. visited section on 14th inst	
" 15th " "	Marched to BAILLEUL and entrained 11 mange cases to ABBEVILLE.	
" 16th " "	Collecting sick	

2

Instructions regarding War Diaries and Intelligence Summaries are contained in F. S. Regs., Part II. and the Staff Manual respectively. Title pages will be prepared in manuscript.

WAR DIARY
or
~~INTELLIGENCE SUMMARY~~.

(*Erase heading not required.*)

Army Form C. 2118.

Hour, Date, Place	Summary of Events and Information	Remarks and references to Appendices
Jan: 17th 1915 BERTHEN	Marched to BAILLEUL and entrained 38 sick horses for NEUFCHATEL.	
" 18th & 19th " "	Collecting sick	
" 20th " "	Marched to BAILLEUL and entrained 15 mange cases to HESDIGNEUL for NEUFCHATEL.	
" 21st " "	Collecting sick	
" 22nd " "	Marched to BAILLEUL and entrained 14 sick horses for NEUFCHATEL	
" 23rd " "	Collecting sick	
" 24th " "	Marched to BAILLEUL and entrained 14 suspected mange cases to HESDIGNEUL for NEUFCHATEL.	
" 25th " "	Collecting sick	
" 26th " "	D.D.V.S. visited section. Marched to ~~??~~ BAILLEUL and entrained 33 sick horses for NEUFCHATEL.	
" 27th & 28th " "	Collecting sick	

3.

Instructions regarding War Diaries and Intelligence Summaries are contained in F. S. Regs., Part II. and the Staff Manual respectively. Title pages will be prepared in manuscript.

WAR DIARY
~~or~~
INTELLIGENCE SUMMARY.
(Erase heading not required.)

Army Form C. 2118.

Hour, Date, Place	Summary of Events and Information	Remarks and references to Appendices
Jany 29th 1915. BERTHEN	Marched to BAILLEUL and entrained 55 ordinary sick cases and 14 mange cases for NEUFCHATEL	
" 30th & 31st " "	Collecting sick –	
	A very wet month and the roads & ground in very bad condition all the time with the exception of 2 or 3 days frost. A large number of cases of Necrosis of the heels (frost bite) admitted & sent away also a great many Debility cases. Found to be impossible to treat these cases satisfactorily under the conditions existing here –	

(9 26 6) W 257—976 100,000 4/12 H W V 79/3298

A.V.D

3rd Division

121
4559.

No 11. Mobile Veterinary Section

Vol XII.

1914

1

Captain W. W. R. Neale AVC
OC. No. XI Mobile Vet. Sectn

Army Form C. 2118.

WAR DIARY
~~or~~
~~INTELLIGENCE~~ SUMMARY.
(*Erase heading not required.*)

Instructions regarding War Diaries and Intelligence Summaries are contained in F. S. Regs., Part II. and the Staff Manual respectively. Title pages will be prepared in manuscript.

Hour, Date, Place	Summary of Events and Information	Remarks and references to Appendices
1.2.15. BERTHEN.	Collecting sick	
2.2.15 "	Marched to BAILLEUL and entrained 30 sick horses for No 10 Veterinary Hospital	
3 & 4-2.15 "	Collecting sick. Visiting units for A.D.V.S. 3rd Div: who had met with an accident the previous day, his horse falling with him.	
5. 2. 15 "	Marched to BAILLEUL and entrained 11 sick horses for No 10 Veterinary Hospital.	
	No 414 Cpl Meecham, H. promoted local temporary Sergeant with pay	
	No 341 Pte Moore, W. promoted to be local temporary paid Lance Corporal	
6, 7 & 8 - 2. 15. "	Collecting sick	
9. 2 15 "	Marched to BAILLEUL and entrained 32 sick horses for No 10 Veterinary Hospital	
10 - 2. 15 " →	No S.E. 767 Pte Heath, A. admitted to Hospital	

2

Captain W. W. R. Neale AVC
OC. No XI Mobile Veterinary Sect

Army Form C. 2118.

WAR DIARY
or
~~INTELLIGENCE~~ SUMMARY.

(Erase heading not required.)

Instructions regarding War Diaries and Intelligence Summaries are contained in F. S. Regs., Part II. and the Staff Manual respectively. Title pages will be prepared in manuscript.

Hour, Date, Place		Summary of Events and Information	Remarks and references to Appendices
11. 2. 1915	BERTHEN.	The D.D.V.S. 2nd Army with the A.D.V.S. inspected the section	
12. 2. 15.	"	Marched to BAILLEUL and entrained 18 sick horses for No 10 Veterinary Hospital.	
13. 2. 15.	"	Received a message from ADVS 3rd Division to go and see him at Head Quarters. Found him in bed with an attack of Influenza and received orders to act as ADVS. of the Division during his illness.	
14 & 15th. 2. 15.	"	~~[illegible]~~ Collecting sick. Performing duties of ADVS.	
16. 2. 15	"	Marched to BAILLEUL and entrained 28 sick horses for No 10 Veterinary Hospital. Performing duties of A.DVS.	
17 - 2. 15	"	Collecting sick and acting for A DVS. No 501 Pte Fawthorpe, F appointed acting Lance Corporal ~~[illegible]~~	

3

Captain W. W. R. Neale AVC
O.C. No XI Mobile Veterinary Sect.

Army Form C. 2118.

Instructions regarding War Diaries and Intelligence Summaries are contained in F. S. Regs., Part II. and the Staff Manual respectively. Title pages will be prepared in manuscript.

WAR DIARY ~~or~~ ~~INTELLIGENCE SUMMARY.~~

(Erase heading not required.)

Hour, Date, Place		Summary of Events and Information	Remarks and references to Appendices
18. 2. 15.	BERTHEN	Collecting sick and acting A.D.V.S.	
19. 2. 15	"	Marched to BAILLEUL and entrained 24 horses (16 sick and 8 pregnant mares) for No 10 Veterinary Hospital. Doing duties of A.D.V.S.	
20. 2. 15	"	A.D.V.S. proceeded on 8 days leave of absence on medical certificate. Received orders to continue officiating for him during his absence.	
21. 2. 15	"	Collecting sick & visiting units	
22. 2. 15	"	D.D.V.S. 2nd Army came to the section and inspected the suspected mange cases under treatment.	
23. 2. 15	"	Marched to BAILLEUL and entrained 29 sick horses for No 10 Veterinary Hospital.	
24 & 25. 2. 15	"	Collecting sick and visiting units.	

4

WAR DIARY ~~or~~ ~~INTELLIGENCE SUMMARY.~~ of Captain W. W. R. Neale A.V.C. O.C. No. XI Mobile Veterinary Sect.

Army Form C. 2118.

Instructions regarding War Diaries and Intelligence Summaries are contained in F. S. Regs., Part II. and the Staff Manual respectively. Title pages will be prepared in manuscript.

(*Erase heading not required.*)

Hour, Date, Place		Summary of Events and Information	Remarks and references to Appendices
26.2.15.	BERTHEN	Marched to BAILLEUL and entrained 11 sick horses for No 10 Veterinary Hospital – D.D.V.S. 2nd Army came to see me at the railway station and gave me orders to place one of our Division Veterinary Officers in charge of the 4th Divisional Ammunition Column billeted at METEREN as Capt O'Rorke A.V.C. who had been in Veterinary charge was leaving and the other 4th Division units were so far away.	
27.2.15	"	Collecting sick & visiting units of the Division	
28.2.15	"	D.D.V.S. returned from leave. With the exception of 6 days 3 – 8 inclusive when it was fine & ground drying nicely, the month was wet with some snow and the ground and roads in very wet, muddy rough order.	

W R Neale / Capt A.V.C.

(9 26 6) W 257—976 100,000 4/12 H W V 79/3298

121/4779

3rd Division

121/4779

11th Mobile Vety Section.

Vol VIIII

March 1915

A.V.D.

1

Instructions regarding War Diaries and Intelligence Summaries are contained in F. S. Regs., Part II. and the Staff Manual respectively. Title pages will be prepared in manuscript.

WAR DIARY ~~or~~ ~~INTELLIGENCE~~ SUMMARY

of Capt. W. R. Neale A.V.C. O.C. XI Mobile Vet: Section

(*Erase heading not required.*)

Army Form C. 2118.

Hour, Date, Place	Summary of Events and Information	Remarks and References to Appendices
March 1st 15 BERTHEN	Collecting sick - Severe snow storm -	
" 2nd " "	Marched to BAILLEUL and entrained 7 mange, 8 other sick and 5 Cast horses for No. 10 Vet: Hospl. NEUFCHATEL. Fine & ground drying up	
" 3rd " "	Collecting sick -	
" 4th " "	Five men joined the section from No. 10 Vet: Hospl.	
" 5th " "	Marched to BAILLEUL and entrained 18 sick horses and 1 board more for No. 10 Vet Hospl.	
" 6th " "	No. 444 Cpl Roberts promoted Sergeant from Jan. 1st 1915. Wet & ground very bad roads.	
" 7th " "	Wet & ground water logged.	
" 8th " "	Collecting sick	
" 9th " "	Marched to BAILLEUL and entrained 17 sick for No. 10 Vet. Hospl. Ground slightly frozen. Snowed in evening	
" 10th " "	Four men joined section from No. 10 Vet: Hospl.	

Instructions regarding War Diaries and Intelligence Summaries are contained in F. S. Regs., Part II. and the Staff Manual respectively. Title pages will be prepared in manuscript.

WAR DIARY ~~or INTELLIGENCE SUMMARY~~

(*Erase heading not required.*)

Capt W. R. Neale A.V.C.
OC. No XI Mobile Vet: Section

Army Form C. 2118.

Hour, Date, Place	Summary of Events and Information	Remarks and References to Appendices
March 11th 1915. BERTHEN	Collecting sick – Reported to A.D.V.S. 3rd Division that the section now over strength in men.	
" 12th " "	Marched to BAILLEUL and entrained 34 sick horses for No 10 Vet: Hospl NEUFCHATEL. Fine & ground drying	
" 13th " "	Routine work.	
" 14th "	Pte Read reported sick and was detained at Hospital. Received orders that surplus personnel of the section to be sent to No 10 Vet: Hospl with next sick horse Conducting party.	
" 15th " "	Collecting sick	
" 16th " "	Marched to BAILLEUL and entrained 18 sick horses + 2 pregnant mares for No 10 Vet: Hospl. – Pte Read discharged from hospital – Surplus personnel of section sent to No 10 Vet: Hospl	

3

WAR DIARY of Capt. W. R. Neale A.V.C. O.C. No XI Mobile Vet: Section

~~or~~

~~INTELLIGENCE SUMMARY~~

(Erase heading not required.)

Army Form C. 2118.

Instructions regarding War Diaries and Intelligence Summaries are contained in F. S. Regs., Part II. and the Staff Manual respectively. Title pages will be prepared in manuscript.

Hour, Date, Place	Summary of Events and Information	Remarks and References to Appendices
March 17th 1915 BERTHEN	D.V.S. accompanied by D.D.V.S. 2nd Army and A.D.V.S. 3rd Division inspected the section.	
" 18 " "	Collecting sick and making microscopic examinations for mange.	
" 19th " "	Marched to BAILLEUL and entrained 23 sick horses and 1 pregnant mare for No 10 Vet: Hospl.	
" 20th " "	No 253 Cpl. C. Moore from 2nd Sergeant } Local Corps order d/16/3/15. " 341 L/Cpl. W. Moore " Corporal " 501 Pte Fawthorpe " Corporal	
	Staff Sergt Manson ordered to No 7 Vet. Hosp. Local Corps order No 10 d/16/3/15.	
" 21st " "	Received orders from A.D.V.S. that Staff Sergt Manson not to proceed to No 7 Vet Hospl but to proceed to WOOLWICH on 22nd inst.	
" 22nd " "	Staff Sergt Manson left section & proceeded to WOOLWICH	

WAR DIARY (4) Capt W. R. Neale A.V.C
XI Mobile Vet: Section

Hour, Date, Place	Summary of Events & Information	Remarks & References to Appx
March 23rd 1915 BERTHEN.	Marched to BAILLEUL and entrained 30 sick horses & 3 pregnant mares for No 10 Vet: Hospl	
" 24th " "	Orders received to transfer No 391 Sergt Clements to No 10 Vet: Hospl	
" 25th " "	Collecting sick	
" 26th " "	Marched to BAILLEUL and entrained 11 sick & 4 mange cases for No 10 Vet: Hospl	
" 27th " "	Proceeded to TERDEGHEM and collected 2 sick horses left with civilian inhabitants.	
" 28th " "	Telegram received by A.D.V.S ordering Lt Sewell to take over the section and for me to proceed to SALISBURY to be an A.D.V.S	
" 29th " "	Handing over to Lt: Sewell A.V.C	
" 31st " "	Left BERTHEN and entrained at BAILLEUL en route for SALISBURY	

W R Neale / Capt A.V.C

121/S 194

3rd. Division

11th Mobile Vety. Section

Vol IX 1–30.4.15

Instructions regarding War Diaries and Intelligence Summaries are contained in F. S. Regs., Part II. and the Staff Manual respectively. Title pages will be prepared in manuscript.

I

WAR DIARY
or
~~INTELLIGENCE SUMMARY.~~

(*Erase heading not required.*)

Army Form C. 2118.

E. Sewell
Lt. AVC
O.C. XI Mobile Veterinary Section

Hour, Date, Place	Summary of Events and Information	Remarks and references to Appendices
1/4/15. Berthen.	Admitting sick.	
2/4/15 "	The Section marched to Bailleul, & entrained 16 horses for No. X Veterinary Hospital.	
3/4/15 "	No. 4936 Private J. Johnson X Hussars attached to No. XI M.V.S., admitted to hospital at Berthen.	
4/4/15 "	at Berthen	
5/4/15 "	Admitting sick.	
6/4/15 "	Section marched to Bailleul & entrained 30 horses for No. X Veterinary Hospital.	
7/4/15 "	No. 3578 Private J. Squires detained in Hospital.	
8/4/15 " Admitting sick	No. 25927 Driver E. Winslade A.S.C. attached No. XI M.V.S. admitted to Hospital, & sent to the Base.	
9/4/15 "	at Berthen.	
10/4/15 "	at Berthen.	
11/4/15 " →	No. 3578 Private J. Squires discharged from Hospital.	
12/4/15 "	Admitting sick.	
13/4/15 "	The Section marched to Bailleul & entrained 25 sick horses for No. X Veterinary Hospital	

(9 29 6) W 4141—463 100,000 9/14 H W V Forms/C. 2118/10

Instructions regarding War Diaries and Intelligence Summaries are contained in F. S. Regs., Part II. and the Staff Manual respectively. Title pages will be prepared in manuscript.

II

WAR DIARY
or
~~INTELLIGENCE SUMMARY.~~
(*Erase heading not required.*)

Army Form C. 2118.

E. Bovell
Lt. A.V.C.
O.C. XI Mobile Veterinary Section

Hour, Date, Place	Summary of Events and Information	Remarks and references to Appendices
14/4/15. Berthen.	Section marched from Berthen at 10 A.M. & arrived at Billet in Westoutre at 11:15 A.M.	
15/4/15 Westoutre.	At Westoutre admitting sick.	
16/4/15 "	Collected Mule from farm at Boeschepe. No. 4936 Private J. Johnson X Hussars attached to No. XI M.V.S. discharged from Hospital. The Section marched to Bailleul & entrained 21 sick horses for No. X Veterinary Hospital.	
17/4/15 "	At Westoutre.	
18/4/15 "	No. 25192 Driver R. McDonald A.S.C. joined Section, to replace Driver E. Winslade.	
19/4/15 "	Admitting sick.	
20/4/15 "	Section marched to Bailleul & entrained 13 sick horses for No. X Veterinary Hospital.	
21/4/15 "	At Westoutre.	
22/4/15 "	Admitting sick.	
23/4/15 "	Section marched to Bailleul & entrained 20 horses for No. X Veterinary Hospital.	

Instructions regarding War Diaries and Intelligence Summaries are contained in F. S. Regs., Part II. and the Staff Manual respectively. Title pages will be prepared in manuscript.

III

WAR DIARY
~~or~~
~~INTELLIGENCE~~ SUMMARY.

(*Erase heading not required.*)

Army Form C. 2118.

E. Powell
Lt. A.V.C.
O.C. XI Mobile Veterinary Section

Hour, Date, Place	Summary of Events and Information	Remarks and references to Appendices
24/4/15. Westoutre	at Westoutre.	
25/4/15 "	at Westoutre.	
26/4/15 "	Admitting sick.	
27/4/15 "	Section marched to Bailleul & entrained 23 sick horses for No. 8 Veterinary Hospital.	
28/4/15 "	at Westoutre.	
29/4/15 "	at Westoutre admitting sick.	
30/4/15 "	At Westoutre. Month dry, & ground in good condition.	

(9 29 6) W 4141—463 100,000 9/14 H W V Forms/C. 2118/10

121/5481

3rd Division.

No 11. Mobile Vety Section

Vol X 1 – 31.5.15.

AVD

Instructions regarding War Diaries and Intelligence Summaries are contained in F. S. Regs., Part II. and the Staff Manual respectively. Title pages will be prepared in manuscript.

I WAR DIARY of No. XI Mobile Veterinary Section

~~INTELLIGENCE SUMMARY.~~

(*Erase heading not required.*)

E. Sewell Lt. A.V.C.

Army Form C. 2118.

Hour, Date, Place	Summary of Events and Information	Remarks and references to Appendices
At Lestouthe 1/5/15	Collecting Sick. 19 horses under treatment.	
" 2/5/15	Collecting Sick. 19 horses under treatment.	
" 3/5/15	Collecting Sick. 13 horses admitted 32 horses under treatment	
" 4/5/15	Section marched to Bailleul & entrained 25 sick horses for No. X Veterinary Hospital. 2 horses re-issued and. 5 Horses remaining under treatment.	
" 5/5/15	Collecting Sick. 5 Horses under treatment.	
" 6/5/15	Admitted 13 sick horses. 18 horses under treatment.	
" 7/5/15	Section marched to Bailleul & entrained 13 sick horses for No. X Veterinary Hospital. No. 255 Sgt. C. Moore transferred to Ambala Cavalry Brigade Mobile Veterinary Section, 5 horses remaining.	
" 8/5/15	Collecting Sick 5 horses remaining.	
" 9/5/15	Collecting Sick. 5 horses remaining.	
" 10/5/15	Admitted 16 horses, 21 remaining	
" 11/5/15	Section marched to Bailleul & entrained 17 horses for No. X Veterinary Hospital. 4 horses remaining	
" 12/5/15	Collecting Sick. 4 horses remaining.	
" 13/5/15	Admitting Sick. 14 horses admitted, 18 horses remaining	

(9 29 6) W4141—463 100,000 9/14 H W V Forms/C. 2118/10

II

Army Form C. 2118.

Instructions regarding War Diaries and Intelligence Summaries are contained in F. S. Regs., Part II. and the Staff Manual respectively. Title pages will be prepared in manuscript.

WAR DIARY of No. XI Mobile Veterinary Section.
or
~~INTELLIGENCE SUMMARY.~~
(Erase heading not required.)

Elwell Lt. A.V.C.

Hour, Date, Place		Summary of Events and Information	Remarks and references to Appendices
[illegible]	14/5/15	Section marched to Bailleul & entrained 15 horses for No. X Veterinary Hospital. 3 horses remaining.	
"	15/5/15	Collecting horses. One horse admitted, 4 horses remaining.	
"	16/5/15	Collecting horses. One horse admitted 5 horses remaining	
"	17/5/15	Admitting Sick. 22 horses admitted. 27 horses remaining	
"	18/5/15	Section marched to Bailleul & entrained 22 horses for No. X Veterinary Hospital.	
"	19/5/15	Collecting Sick. 5 horses remaining.	
"	20/5/15	Admitting Sick. 9 horses admitted. 14 horses remaining.	
"	21/5/15	Collecting Sick. 3 horses admitted. 17 horses remaining.	
"	22/5/15	Collecting Sick. 17 horses remaining.	
"	23/5/15	Collecting Sick. 17 horses remaining.	
"	24/5/15	Admitting Sick. 10 horses admitted. 27 remaining.	
"	25/5/15	Section marched to Bailleul & entrained 16 horses for No. X Veterinary Hospital. 11 horses remaining.	
"	26/5/15	Collecting Sick. 4 horses admitted. 15 horses remaining.	
"	27/5/15	Admitting Sick. 19 horses admitted. 34 horses remaining	
"	28/5/15	Section marched to Bailleul & entrained 22 horses & 2 Mares with foals at foot to No X Veterinary Hospital. 10 Horses remaining.	
"	29/5/15	Collecting Sick. No. 1960 Pte. Clissold H. No. 3017 Pte Judd J. No. 3254 Pte. Belcher G.J. joined the section from No. 6 Veterinary Hospital. 10 Horses remaining.	

(9 29 6) W4141—463 100,000 9/14 H W V Forms/C. 2118/10

III

Army Form C. 2118.

WAR DIARY of No. XI Mobile Veterinary Section

~~or~~

~~INTELLIGENCE SUMMARY.~~

(*Erase heading not required.*)

E Lewell Lt. A.V.C.

Instructions regarding War Diaries and Intelligence Summaries are contained in F. S. Regs., Part II. and the Staff Manual respectively. Title pages will be prepared in manuscript.

Hour, Date, Place	Summary of Events and Information	Remarks and references to Appendices
at Westoutre 30/5/15	Collecting Sect. 10 horses remaining	
" 31/5/15	Admitting Sect. 16 horses admitted. Section moved into new Billet in Commune of Westoutre at 10 A.M. 26 horses remaining.	

(9 29 6) W4141—463 100,000 9/14 H W V Forms/C. 2118/10

3rd Division

181/5993

No 11 Mobile Vety: Section

Vol XI. 1 — 30.6.15

Instructions regarding War Diaries and Intelligence Summaries are contained in F. S. Regs., Part II. and the Staff Manual respectively. Title pages will be prepared in manuscript.

I WAR DIARY of No. XI Mobile Veterinary Section 3rd Division

or

~~INTELLIGENCE SUMMARY.~~

(*Erase heading not required.*)

Army Form C. 2118.

E. Powell Capt. AVC
O.C. XI Mobile Veterinary Section

Hour, Date, Place	Summary of Events and Information	Remarks and references to Appendices
1/6/15 at Westoutre	Section marched to Bailleul & entrained 17 sick horses for No. X Veterinary Hospital. 9 sick horses remaining	
2/6/15 "	Collecting sick. Admitted 3 sick horses, 12 sick horses remaining	
3/6/15 "	Collecting sick. Admitted 10 sick horses, 22 sick horses remaining	
4/6/15 "	Section marched at 10 A.M. & arrived at new Billet 10:30 A.M. 1 sick horse admitted, 23 sick horses remaining	
5/6/15 "	Section marched at 7 A.M. & arrived at billets in Poperinghe at 7:30 A.M. Section marched to Godewaersvelde at 10 A.M. & entrained 12 sick horses for No. X Veterinary Hospital. 11 sick horses remaining.	
6/6/15 Poperinghe	Collecting sick, 11 sick horses remaining	
7/6/15 "	Collecting sick. 10 sick horses admitted. 21 sick horses remaining	
8/6/15 "	Section marched to Godewaersvelde, & entrained 7 sick horses & 1 mare with foal at foot to No. X Veterinary Hospital. 5 sick horses admitted. 1 re-issued unit. 12 sick horses remaining.	
9/6/15 "	Collecting sick. Admitted 7 sick horses, 19 sick horses remaining	
10/6/15 "	Collecting sick. Admitted 16 sick horses, 35 sick horses remaining.	

(9 29 6) W4141—463 100,000 9/14 H W V Forms/C. 2118/10

II

WAR DIARY of No. XI Mobile Veterinary Section 3rd Division

~~or~~

~~INTELLIGENCE~~ SUMMARY.

(Erase heading not required.)

Army Form C. 2118.

Instructions regarding War Diaries and Intelligence Summaries are contained in F. S. Regs., Part II. and the Staff Manual respectively. Title pages will be prepared in manuscript.

E. Sewell Capt. A.V.C.
O.C. XI Mobile Veterinary Section.

Hour, Date, Place	Summary of Events and Information	Remarks and references to Appendices
11/6/15 Poperinghe	Section marched to Godewaersvelde, & entrained 24 sick horses for No. X Veterinary Hospital. 8 sick remaining.	
12/6/15 "	Collecting sick. Admitted 4 sick horses. 12 sick remaining.	
13/6/15 "	Collecting sick. Admitted 1 sick horse. 13 sick remaining.	
14/6/15 "	Collecting sick. 19 sick admitted. 34 sick remaining.	
15/6/15 "	Section marched to Godewaersvelde & entrained 18 sick horses, 3 Mange, & 1 Mare with foal at foot. 12 sick remaining.	
16/6/15 "	Collecting sick. An advanced aid Post was established near Ypres, consisting of 1 N.C.O. & 3 Men. 4 wounded horses admitted. 16 sick remaining.	
17/6/15 "	Collecting sick. 8 sick horses admitted. advanced aid Post withdrawn. 24 sick remaining.	
18/6/15 "	Section marched to Poperinghe & entrained 13 sick horses + 1 Mare with foal at foot to No. X Veterinary Hospital. 10 sick remaining.	
19/6/15 "	Collecting sick. admitted 1 sick horse. 11 sick remaining. The G.O.C. 2nd Army inspected the section at 3.30 P.M.	
20/6/15 "	Collecting sick. 3 horses returned cured. 8 sick remaining.	
21/6/15 "	Collecting sick. admitted 19 sick. 27 sick remaining.	
22/6/15 "	Section marched to Poperinghe & entrained 20 sick horses for No. X Veterinary Hospital. 2 horses destroyed. [illegible] returned cured. 11 sick remaining.	

Instructions regarding War Diaries and Intelligence Summaries are contained in F. S. Regs., Part II. and the Staff Manual respectively. Title pages will be prepared in manuscript.

III

WAR DIARY of No. XI Mobile Veterinary Section 3rd Division

~~or~~

~~INTELLIGENCE SUMMARY.~~

(Erase heading not required.)

Army Form C. 2118.

E Lovell Lt AVC
O.C. XI Mobile Veterinary Section.

Hour, Date, Place	Summary of Events and Information	Remarks and references to Appendices
23/6/15 Poperinghe	Collecting Sick. 1 horse destroyed. 15 sick remaining.	
24/6/15 "	Collecting sick. Admitted 21 sick horses. 31 sick remaining	
25/6/15 "	Section marched to Poperinghe & entrained 19 sick horses & 3 cases Mange to No. X Veterinary Hospital. 1 horse admitted, 1 re-mount cured. 9 sick remaining	
26/6/15 "	Collecting sick. 3 horses admitted. 13 sick remaining.	
27/6/15 "	Collecting sick. Admitted 2 sick horses. 15 sick remaining.	
28/6/15 "	Collecting sick. Admitted 8 sick horses. 23 sick horses remaining	
29/6/15 "	Section marched to Poperinghe & entrained 9 sick horses, 1 pregnant Mare & 14 Cast Horses to No. X Veterinary Hospital. 5 horses re-mount cured. 10 sick remaining. No 497 Pte Lewis J appointed Acting Lance Corporal. 10 sick remaining.	
30/6/15	Collecting sick. Admitted 2 sick horses. 12 sick horses remaining.	

3rd Division

121/6243

No 11 Mobile Vety: Section

Vol XII

1-31-4-15

Instructions regarding War Diaries and Intelligence Summaries are contained in F. S. Regs., Part II. and the Staff Manual respectively. Title pages will be prepared in manuscript.

WAR DIARY of No. XI Mobile Veterinary Section 3rd Division.
~~or~~
~~INTELLIGENCE SUMMARY.~~
(Erase heading not required.)

I.

Army Form C. 2118.

E. Powell Lt. A.V.C.
O.C. XI Mobile Veterinary Section

Hour, Date, Place	Summary of Events and Information	Remarks and references to Appendices
1/7/15 Poperinghe	Admitting sick. 10 sick horses admitted. 23 horses remaining.	
2/7/15. "	Admitting sick. 4 horses re-issued. 19 horses remaining.	
3/7/15 "	Admitting sick. 1 sick horse admitted. 20 horses remaining	
4/7/15 "	Admitting sick. 20 sick horses remaining.	
5/7/15 "	Admitting sick. 7 sick horses admitted. 27 horses remaining	
6/7/15 "	The section marched to Poperinghe, & evacuated 14 ordinary sick, & 2 cases of mange to Advanced Veterinary Hospital. 3 horses re-issued. 8 horses remaining.	
7/7/15 "	Admitting sick. 2 suspected Mange admitted. 10 horses remaining.	
8/7/15 "	Admitting sick. 9 sick horses admitted. 19 horses remaining.	
9/7/15 "	As inhabitants in billet had contracted Enteric fever, Section moved to adjacent billet. 1 susp. Mange admitted. 20 horses remaining.	
10/7/15 "	Admitting sick. 1 horse admitted. 21 horses remaining.	
11/7/15 "	Admitting sick. 2 horses admitted. ~~W~~ 23 horses remaining.	
12/7/15 "	Admitting sick. 11 horses admitted. 2 horses re-issued. 32 horses remaining.	

Instructions regarding War Diaries and Intelligence Summaries are contained in F. S. Regs., Part II. and the Staff Manual respectively. Title pages will be prepared in manuscript.

WAR DIARY of No. XI Mobile Veterinary Section 5th Division

~~or~~

~~INTELLIGENCE SUMMARY.~~ II.

(*Erase heading not required.*)

Army Form C. 2118.

E. Sewell Capt. AVC
O.C. XI Mobile Veterinary Section

Hour, Date, Place	Summary of Events and Information	Remarks and references to Appendices
13/7/15 Poperinghe.	Section marched to Poperinghe & entrained 20 sick horses & 2 cases Mange to Advanced Veterinary Hospital. 3 sick & 1 susp. Mange admitted. 14 horses remaining	
14/7/15 "	Collecting sick. 14 horses remaining.	
15/7/15 "	Admitting sick 19 sick horses admitted. 33 horses remaining	
16/7/15 "	Section marched to Poperinghe & entrained 17 sick for advanced Veterinary Hospital. 1 sick horse & 1 susp. Mange admitted. 18 horses remaining.	
17/7/15 "	Admitting sick. 1 horse admitted. 19 horses remaining.	
18/7/15 "	Admitted 3 sick. 1 horse re-issued. 18 horses remaining.	
19/7/15 "	Admitting sick. 14 sick horses admitted. 35 horses remaining.	
20/7/15 "	Admitting sick. 10 sick horses admitted. 4 horses re-issued. 41 horses remaining.	
21/7/15 "	Admitting sick 1 susp. Mange admitted. 42 horses remaining.	
22/7/15 "	Section marched to Poperinghe & entrained 24 sick horses for advanced Veterinary Hospital. 5 sick horses & 1 case susp. Mange admitted. 24 horses remaining.	
~~[illegible]~~ 23/7/15 "	Admitting sick. 1 sick horse admitted. 1 horse re-issued. 24 horses remaining	
24/7/15 "	Admitting sick. 9 sick horses admitted. 33 horses remaining.	

Instructions regarding War Diaries and Intelligence Summaries are contained in F. S. Regs., Part II. and the Staff Manual respectively. Title pages will be prepared in manuscript.

WAR DIARY of XI Mobile Veterinary Section 32nd Division
or
~~INTELLIGENCE~~ SUMMARY. III

(*Erase heading not required.*)

Army Form C. 2118.

E. Sewell Lt. A.V.C.
O.C. XI Mobile Veterinary Section

Hour, Date, Place	Summary of Events and Information	Remarks and references to Appendices
25/7/15 Poperinghe.	Admitting Sick. 11 Sick horses admitted. 2 horses re-issued. 42 horses remaining.	
26/7/15 "	Admitting Sick. 16 Sick horses admitted. 58 horses remaining.	
27/7/15 "	Section Marched to Poperinghe & entrained 32 Sick horses & 1 Pregnant Mare for Advanced Veterinary Hospital. 25 horses remaining.	
28/7/15 "	Admitting Sick. 8 horses admitted. 5 horses re-issued. 31 horses remaining.	
29/7/15 "	Admitting Sick. 16 Sick & 17 horses cast by D.D.R. 2nd Army admitted. Major General Winter, D.A. & Q.M.G. 2nd Army. Visited Section, inspected it. 59 horses remaining.	
30/7/15 "	Section marched to Poperinghe & entrained 39 horses for advanced Veterinary Hospital. 1 horse re-issued. 19 horses remaining.	
31/7/15 "	Admitting Sick. 1 horse admitted. 20 horses remaining	

3rd Division

121/6607

No 11 Mobile Vety: Section

Vol XIII

From 1 – 31 – 8. 15

RVP

Instructions regarding War Diaries and Intelligence Summaries are contained in F. S. Regs., Part II. and the Staff Manual respectively. Title pages will be prepared in manuscript.

WAR DIARY I

~~or~~ ~~INTELLIGENCE~~ SUMMARY.

of No. XI Mobile Veterinary Section 3rd Division.

(*Erase heading not required.*)

Army Form C. 2118.

E. Sewell Lt. Avc.
O.C. XI M.V.S.

Hour, Date, Place	Summary of Events and Information	Remarks and references to Appendices
1/8/15 Poperinghe	Collecting sick. 28 sick remaining.	
2/8/15 "	Collecting sick. admitted 25. 53 sick horses remaining.	
3/8/15 "	Section marched to Poperinghe & entrained 30 sick horses to No. 8 Veterinary Hospital. Re-issued 1 horse cured, & admitted 2. 24 sick horses remaining	
4/8/15 "	Collecting sick. 2 horses admitted. 26 sick horses remaining.	
5/8/15 "	Collecting sick. 19 horses admitted. 45 horses remaining.	
6/8/15 "	Section marched to Poperinghe & entrained 8 Cast horses, 3 Cases mange, & 15 ordinary sick to Advanced Veterinary Hospital. 12 horses admitted, & 1 destroyed. 27 horses remaining.	
7/8/15 "	Collecting sick. 2 horses admitted, 1 re-issued cured, 28 horses remaining	
8/8/15 "	Collecting sick admitted 1. 29 horses remaining	
9/8/15 "	Collecting sick admitted 11 sick horses, re-issued 1 cured. 40 remaining.	
10/8/15 "	Section marched to Poperinghe & entrained 5 Cast horses, 3 Cases Mange, & 8 ordinary sick to Advanced Veterinary Hospital. 2 sick horses admitted. 23 horses remaining.	

(9 29 6) W4141—463 100,000 9/14 H W V Forms/C. 2118/10

II

Army Form C. 2118.

Instructions regarding War Diaries and Intelligence Summaries are contained in F. S. Regs., Part II. and the Staff Manual respectively. Title pages will be prepared in manuscript.

WAR DIARY of No. XI Mobile Veterinary Section 3rd Division
~~or~~
~~INTELLIGENCE SUMMARY.~~

(Erase heading not required.)

E. Lowell Lt. AVC.
OC. XI M. V. S.

Hour, Date, Place	Summary of Events and Information	Remarks and references to Appendices
11/8/15 Poperinghe	Collecting sick. 4 sick horses admitted. 27 horses remaining	
12/8/15 "	Collecting sick. 17 sick horses admitted. 1 horse re-issued cured. 43 horses remaining.	
13/8/15 "	Section marched to Poperinghe & entrained 19 sick horses for advanced Veterinary Hospital. 24 horses remaining	
14/8/15 "	Collecting sick 2 sick horses admitted. 6 horses re-issued cured. 19 sick horses remaining.	
15/8/15 "	Collecting sick. 1 horse admitted 20 Horses remaining	
16/8/15 "	Collecting sick. 11 sick horses admitted 1 horse re-issued cured. 30 sick horses remaining.	
17/8/15 "	Section marched to Poperinghe, & entrained 12 sick horses, & 1 Case of Mange to advanced Veterinary Hospital 17 sick horses remaining.	
18/8/15 "	Collecting sick. 4 sick horses admitted, re-issued 1 horse cured. 20 sick horses remaining.	
19/8/15 "	Collecting sick. 22 sick horses admitted. 42 horses remaining.	
20/8/15 "	Section marched to Poperinghe, & entrained 21 ordinary sick, & 2 cases Mange to advanced Veterinary Hospital 1 horse died, & 2 destroyed. 1 horse admitted 16 horses remaining	

(9 29 6) W4141—463 100,000 9/14 H W V Forms/C. 2118/10

Instructions regarding War Diaries and Intelligence Summaries are contained in F. S. Regs., Part II. and the Staff Manual respectively. Title pages will be prepared in manuscript.

III

Army Form C. 2118.

WAR DIARY ~~or~~ ~~INTELLIGENCE~~ ~~SUMMARY~~. of No. XI Mobile Veterinary Section 3rd Division

(Erase heading not required.)

E. Sewell Cp. AVC. OC. XI M.V.S.

Hour, Date, Place	Summary of Events and Information	Remarks and references to Appendices
21/8/15 Poperinghe.	Collecting Sick. 1 horse admitted. 1 horse died, & 1 horse reissued cured. 15 Sick horses remaining.	
22/8/15 "	Collecting Sick. 3 horses re-issued cured. 1 horse 17th Division admitted. No. 949 S.S. W. KEEN admitted to hospital. 13 horses remaining.	
23/8/15 "	Collecting Sick, 30 horses admitted. 1 horse died, & 1 horse (17th Division) Destroyed. 41 horses remaining. S.E. No. 2132 Pte. A WATSON admitted to hospital.	
~~24/8~~ 24/8/15 "	Section marched to Poperinghe, & entrained 20 Cast horses & 12 Sick to Advanced Veterinary Hospital. 4 Sick horses admitted. 2 horses reissued cured. 11 horses remaining.	
25/8/15 "	Collecting Sick. 3 horses admitted. 2 horses reissued Cured 12 Sick horses remaining.	
26/8/15 "	Collecting Sick. 14 Sick horses admitted. 1 horse re-issued cured. 25 Sick horses remaining.	
27/8/15 "	Section marched to Poperinghe, & entrained 12 Sick horses for advanced Veterinary Hospital. 1 Sick horse admitted, 13 Sick horses remaining. S.E. No 2132 Pte. A. WATSON discharged from Hospital.	
28/8/15 "	Collecting Sick. 1 horse admitted S.E. No. 4320 S.S. G. WADDELL Joined the Section from No. 2 Veterinary Hospital. 14 horses remaining	
29/8/15 "	Collecting Sick. 14 horses remaining.	
30/8/15 "	Collecting Sick 14 horses remaining	
31/8/15 "	Collecting Sick. 3 horses admitted. 17 Sick horses remaining	

(9 29 6) W4141—463 100,000 9/14 H W V Forms/C. 2118/10

File

3rd Division

121/7051

No 11 Mobile Vety: Section

Vol XIV

Sep 15

Instructions regarding War Diaries and Intelligence Summaries are contained in F. S. Regs., Part II. and the Staff Manual respectively. Title pages will be prepared in manuscript.

WAR DIARY of No. 7 Mobile Veterinary Section
or
~~INTELLIGENCE SUMMARY.~~
(Erase heading not required.)

No. 7 3rd Division

Army Form C. 2118.

E. Sewell Lt. A.V.C.
O.C. 7 M.V.S.

Hour, Date, Place	Summary of Events and Information	Remarks and references to Appendices
1/9/15 Poperinghe	Collecting Sick. 21 horses admitted. 41 horses remaining	
2/9/15 "	Collecting Sick. 3 horses admitted, 3 re-issued Cured. 1 horse destroyed 40 sick horses remaining.	
3/9/15 "	Section marched to Poperinghe & entrained 27 horses for Advanced Veterinary Hospital. 1 horse admitted. 14 horses remaining	
4/9/15 "	Collecting Sick 1 horse admitted 2 horses re-issued Cured. 13 horses remaining.	
5/9/15 "	Collecting Sick. 1 horse admitted 1 horse re-issued Cured. 13 horses remaining. No 4197 Pte. Laws J. proceeded to England on leave	
~~[illegible]~~ "	S.E. No 659 Pte. RANGERT rejoined the Section from leave.	
6/9/15 "	Collecting Sick. 2 horses admitted 15 horses remaining.	
7/9/15 "	Collecting Sick 2 horses admitted. 17 horses remaining.	
8/9/15 "	Collecting Sick. 15 horses admitted. 1 horse destroyed. 1 horse re-issued 30 horses remaining.	
9/9/15 "	Collecting Sick. 1 horse admitted. 31 horses remaining	
10/9/15 "	Section marched to Poperinghe & entrained 24 horses to Advanced Veterinary Hospital. 8 horses remaining.	
11/9/15 "	Collecting Sick. 1 horse admitted. 9 horses remaining	
12/9/15 "	Collecting Sick 2 horses admitted. 1 horse re-issued 10 horses remaining	

Instructions regarding War Diaries and Intelligence Summaries are contained in F. S. Regs., Part II. and the Staff Manual respectively. Title pages will be prepared in manuscript.

Army Form C. 2118.

WAR DIARY of XI Mobile Veterinary Section 3rd Division
or
~~INTELLIGENCE SUMMARY.~~
II
(*Erase heading not required.*)

E. Lewell Lt. A.V.C. O.C. XI M.V.S.

Hour, Date, Place	Summary of Events and Information	Remarks and references to Appendices
13/9/15. Poperinghe	Collecting Sick. 4 horses admitted. No. SE. 2526 Pte. Busby A. admitted to hospital. 14 horses remaining.	
14/9/15 "	Collecting Sick. 14 horses remaining.	
15/9/15 "	Collecting Sick. 15 horses admitted. 1 horse reissued cured. 25 horses remaining.	
16/9/15 "	Collecting Sick. 3 horses admitted. 31 horses remaining.	
17/9/15 "	Section marched to Poperinghe, & entrained 21 horses to Advanced Veterinary Hospital. 3 horses admitted. 3 horses re-issued cured. 10 horses remaining.	
18/9/15 "	Collecting Sick. No. 341 Corp. MOORE W. admitted to hospital. 10 horses remaining.	
19/9/15 "	Collecting Sick. 3 horses admitted. 2 reissued cured. 10 horses remaining. Nos. T. 111 Pte. UNDERHILL W. & T. 116 Pte. HARRIS A. joined the Section from No. 2 Veterinary Hospital. 11 horses remaining.	
20/9/15 "	Collecting Sick. 1 horse admitted. 1 horse re-issued. 11 horses remaining.	
21/9/15 "	Collecting Sick. 1 horse admitted. 1 horse destroyed. No. 25792 Dr. McDONALD R. Proceeded to Scotland on leave. 11 horses remaining.	
22/9/15 "	Collecting Sick. 22 horses admitted. 1 reissued. 32 horses remaining. No. 341 Sgt. Moore W. discharged from hospital. No. 341 Corp. Moore W. was promoted to the rank of Temp. Sergt. with pay, from 12/9/15.	

Instructions regarding War Diaries and Intelligence Summaries are contained in F. S. Regs., Part II. and the Staff Manual respectively. Title pages will be prepared in manuscript.

WAR DIARY of [illegible] XI Mobile Veterinary Section 3rd Division
111

or

~~INTELLIGENCE SUMMARY.~~

(*Erase heading not required.*)

Army Form C. 2118.

E. Jewell Lt. A.V.C. O.C. XI M.V.S.

Hour, Date, Place	Summary of Events and Information	Remarks and references to Appendices
23/9/15 Poperinghe	Collecting Sect. 29 horses admitted. 61 horses remaining. Nos T.111 Ptes UNDERHILL W & T116 Pte HARRIS A. posted to join the 48th Division Mobile Veterinary Section.	
24/9/15 "	Section marched to Poperinghe & entrained 49 horses for advanced Veterinary Hospital. 3 horses re-issued. 11 horses remaining.	
25/9/15 "	Collecting Sect. At 5 P.M. The O.C. & 7 men marched to [illegible] Chateau near Ypres & established an advanced Aid Post. 11 horses remaining.	
26/9/15 "	Collecting Sect. 1 horse admitted, 12 horses remaining. Advanced Aid Post came under shell fire, & changed its quarters to Kruisstraat.	
27/9/15 "	Collecting Sect 1 horse admitted. Advanced Aid Post was withdrawn & rejoined the Section. 13 horses remaining.	
28/9/15 "	Collecting Sect. 1 horse admitted 1 horse received cured. 13 horses remaining.	
29/9/15 "	Collecting Sect. 9 horses admitted 22 horses remaining. No. 25792 Pte. McDONALD R rejoined the Section from leave.	
30/9/15 "	Collecting Sect. 1 horse admitted, 23 horses remaining.	

3

11th Mob. Vet. Sec.

Oct

Vol. XV

121/7929

Copy

Instructions regarding War Diaries and Intelligence Summaries are contained in F. S. Regs., Part II. and the Staff Manual respectively. Title pages will be prepared in manuscript.

WAR DIARY of No. XI Mobile Veterinary Section 3rd Division or ~~INTELLIGENCE SUMMARY.~~

(*Erase heading not required.*)

No. I

Army Form C. 2118.

by E. Powell H.A.V.C. O.C. XI M.V.S.

Hour, Date, Place	Summary of Events and Information	Remarks and references to Appendices
In the field. 1. 10. 15	Section marched to Poperinghe & entrained 9 horses for advanced Veterinary Hospital 14 horses remaining.	
At Poperinghe 2. 10. 15	Collecting Sick. 2 sick horses admitted. 2 horses reissued cured. S.E. No. 1205 Pte. LAING.W. & S.E. No. 5075 TINSON W. joined this Section from No. 29 Mobile Veterinary Section 17th Division.	
" 3. 10. 15.	14 horses remaining. Collecting Sick. 3 horses admitted. 3 horses re-issued cured. 14 horses remaining. No. S.E. 1960 Pte. CLISSOLD.H. reported detained under arrest at Boulogne.	
" 4. 10. 15	Collecting Sick. Section Practice at Rifle Range. S.E. No. 1960 Pte. CLISSOLD. H. rejoined Section, 14 horses remaining.	
" 5. 10. 15.	Collecting Sick. 1 horse admitted. 1 horse re-issued cured. 14 horses remaining.	
" 6. 10. 15	Collecting Sick. 11 horses admitted. 1 reissued cured. 1 horse destroyed. S.E. No. 1960. Pte. CLISSOLD H. Awarded 21 days field Punishment No. 1. 23 horses remaining. Section was inspected by D.D.R. 2nd Army.	
" 7. 10. 15	Collecting Sick. 4 horses admitted. 27 horses remaining. No. 25192 Dr. MacDonald R. admitted to hospital, & evacuated.	
" 8. 10. 15	Collecting Sick. 3 horses admitted. Section marched to Poperinghe & entrained 14 horses for advanced Veterinary Hospital. 2 horses reissued cured. 14 horses remaining.	
" 9. 10. 15	Collecting Sick. 1 horse reissued cured. 13 horses remaining.	
" 10. 10. 15	Collecting Sick. 1 horse died. S.E. No. 1205 Pte. LAING W. admitted to hospital, & evacuated.	

(9 29 6) W4141—463 100,000 9/14 H W V Forms/C. 2118/10

Army Form C. 2118.

Instructions regarding War Diaries and Intelligence Summaries are contained in F. S. Regs., Part II. and the Staff Manual respectively. Title pages will be prepared in manuscript.

WAR DIARY
or
INTELLIGENCE SUMMARY.
(*Erase heading not required.*)

of No. II Mobile Veterinary Section 3rd Division by E. Lovell Lt. A.V.C. O.C. II M.V.S.

No. 2.

Hour, Date, Place	Summary of Events and Information	Remarks and references to Appendices
At Poperinghe. 11. 10. 15	Collecting Sick. 12 horses remaining	
" 12. 10. 15	Collecting Sick. 27 horses admitted. 39 horses remaining. S.E. No 833 Pte. JONES A. proceeded to England on leave.	
" 13. 10. 15	Collecting Sick. 4 horses admitted. 43 horses remaining.	
" 14. 10. 15	Collecting Sick. 3 horses admitted. 27 Sick & 1 Cast horse evacuated to No. Advanced Veterinary Hospital. 2 horses reissued cured. 16 horses remaining. No. 497 Pte. LAWS J. promoted Corporal, authority Base Corps orders. No. 36. G.H.Q. 3rd Echelon. 11. 10. 15.	
" 15. 10. 15	Collecting Sick. 2 horses admitted. 3 re-issued cured. 15 horses remaining.	
" 16. 10. 15	Collecting Sick. 15 horses remaining	
" 17. 10. 15.	Collecting Sick. 1 horse admitted. 1 horse reissued cured. 15 horses remaining.	
" 18. 10. 15	Collecting Sick. 15 horses remaining.	
" 19. 10. 15.	Collecting Sick. 15 horses remaining.	
" 20. 10. 15	Collecting Sick. 24 horses admitted. 1 horse re-issued cured. 1 horse destroyed. 37 horses remaining. No. S.E 833 Pte. JONES A. returned from leave.	
" 21. 10. 15	Collecting Sick. 8 horses admitted. 3 horses re-issued cured. 42 horses remaining.	
" 22. 10. 15	Collecting Sick. 7 horses admitted 1 horse re-issued cured. Station transferred to Poperinghe & evacuated 38 sick for Advanced Veterinary Hospital. 10 horses remaining	

(9 29 6) W4141—463 100,000 9/14 H W V Forms/C. 2118/10

Instructions regarding War Diaries and Intelligence Summaries are contained in F. S. Regs., Part II. and the Staff Manual respectively. Title pages will be prepared in manuscript.

Army Form C. 2118.

WAR DIARY
or ~~INTELLIGENCE SUMMARY.~~
(*Erase heading not required.*)

of No. 11 Mobile Veterinary Section. 3rd Division by E. Lovell Lt. A.V.C. O.C. 11. M. V. S.

No. 3.

Hour, Date, Place	Summary of Events and Information	Remarks and references to Appendices
at Poperinghe 23.10.15	Collecting Sick. 10 horses remaining. S.E. No 687 Pte. PETTITT J. admitted to hospital & evacuated.	
Steenvoorde 24.10.15	Section Marched from Poperinghe, & took over rest Billets from No. 29 M.V.S. at STEENVOORDE. 3 horses left with No. 29 M.V.S. 1 horse taken over from No. 29 M.V.S. 17th Division 8 horses remaining.	
" 25.10.15	Collecting Sick. 8 remaining.	
" 26.10.15	Collecting Sick. 1 horse admitted. 9 horses remaining	
" 27.10.15	Collecting Sick. 4 horses admitted. 2 returned cured. 11 horses remaining. 2 N.C.O's & 6 Men joined No. 11 M.V.S. from No. 2 Vety. Hospital.	
" 28.10.15	Collecting Sick. 17 horses admitted. 28 horses remaining. 15 Cast & 6 Sick evacuated to advanced Veterinary Hospital.	
" 29.10.15	Collecting Sick. 3 horses admitted. 2 N.C.O's & 5 men transferred from Section to No. 2 Veterinary Hospital. Section inspected by D.D.V.S. 2nd Army.	
" 30.10.15	Collecting Sick. 5 horses admitted. 15 horses remaining	
" 31.10.15	Collecting Sick. 2 horses admitted. 17 horses remaining	

(9 29 6) W 4141—463 100,000 9/14 H W V Forms/C. 2118/10

3rd Division

3rd Dn

11 Mobile Vet. Sec.

Nov. /

Vol XVI

121/7667

Instructions regarding War Diaries and Intelligence Summaries are contained in F. S. Regs., Part II. and the Staff Manual respectively. Title pages will be prepared in manuscript.

Army Form C. 2118.

No. I

WAR DIARY of [illegible] Mobile Veterinary Section 3rd Division

or

~~INTELLIGENCE SUMMARY.~~

(*Erase heading not required.*)

by E. Sewell Lt. A.V.C.

Hour, Date, Place		Summary of Events and Information	Remarks and references to Appendices
Steenvoorde	1. 11. 15	Collecting sick. 16 horses remaining	
"	2. 11. 15	Collecting sick. 1 sick horse admitted. 17 horses remaining. No. 1012 Pte. JOHNSON. J. admitted to hospital & evacuated.	
"	3. 11. 15	Collecting sick. 13 horses admitted. 1 horse re-issued cured. 29 horses remaining.	
"	4. 11. 15	Collecting sick. 3 sick horses admitted. 1 horse destroyed. 31 horses remaining. No. 880 Pte. JOHNS J. proceeded to England on leave.	
"	5. 11. 15	Collecting sick. 1 horse admitted. 1 horse destroyed. Section marched Cassel & entrained 19 sick & 1 cast horse to Advanced Veterinary Hospital. 11 horses remaining	
"	6. 11. 15	Collecting sick. 3 horses admitted. 14 horses remaining.	
"	7. 11. 15	Collecting sick. 2 horses admitted. 1 horse destroyed. 15 horses remaining.	
"	8. 11. 15	Collecting sick. 1 horse admitted. 16 horses remaining.	
"	9. 11. 15	Collecting sick. 2 horses admitted. 2 horses reissued cured. 16 horses remaining. No. 687 Pte. PETTIT. J. rejoined the section from hospital.	
"	10. 11. 15	Collecting sick. 10 horses admitted. 2 horses re-issued cured. 24 horses remaining	

(9 29 6) W 4141—463 100,000 9/14 H W V Forms/C. 2118/10

No. 2.

Instructions regarding War Diaries and Intelligence Summaries are contained in F. S. Regs., Part II. and the Staff Manual respectively. Title pages will be prepared in manuscript.

WAR DIARY of No. XI Mobile Veterinary Section 3rd Division

~~or~~

~~INTELLIGENCE~~ SUMMARY.

(*Erase heading not required.*)

by E. Sewell Lt. A.V.C.

Army Form C. 2118.

Hour, Date, Place	Summary of Events and Information	Remarks and references to Appendices
Steenvoorde 11. 11. 15	Collecting Sick. 1 horse admitted. 1 horse re-issued cured. Section marched to Caestre & entrained 13 sick for Advanced Veterinary Hospital. 11 horses remaining.	
" 12. 11. 15	Collecting Sick 2 sick horses admitted. 1 horse re-issued cured. 12 horses remaining.	
" 13. 11. 15	Collecting Sick. 3 horses admitted. 15 horses remaining.	
" 14. 11. 15	Collecting Sick. 15 horses remaining.	
" 15. 11. 15	Collecting Sick. 3 horses re-issued cured. 12 horses remaining.	
" 16. 11. 15	Collecting Sick. 1 horse admitted. 13 horses remaining.	
" 17. 11. 15	Collecting Sick. 9 horses admitted. 22 remaining.	
" 18. 11. 15	Collecting Sick. 7 horses admitted. 2 re-issued cured 1 died 26 remaining.	
" 19. 11. 15	Collecting Sick 13 sick admitted. Section marched to Caestre & entrained 16 horses for No. X Veterinary Hospital. 1 horse re-issued cured 22 remaining.	
" 20. 11. 15	Collecting Sick 6 admitted. 3 re-issued cured 25 remaining.	
" 21. 11. 15	Collecting Sick. 3 admitted. Section marched to Caestre & entrained 16 horses for No. X Veterinary Hospital. 12 horses remaining.	

(9 29 6) W4141—463 100,000 9/14 H W V Forms/C. 2118/10

No. 3

Instructions regarding War Diaries and Intelligence Summaries are contained in F. S. Regs., Part II. and the Staff Manual respectively. Title pages will be prepared in manuscript.

WAR DIARY of No. XI Mobile Veterinary Section 3rd Division

or

~~INTELLIGENCE SUMMARY.~~

(Erase heading not required.) by E. Sewell Lt. A.V.C.

Army Form C. 2118.

Hour, Date, Place	Summary of Events and Information	Remarks and references to Appendices
Steenvoorde. 22.11.15	Collecting Sick. 7 admitted. 2 destroyed. 17 remaining	
" 23.11.15	Collecting Sick. 16 admitted 1 died. 32 remaining.	
" 24.11.15	Collecting Sick. 3 admitted. Section marched to Cassel & entrained 24 Sick for No. X Veterinary Hospital. 11 remaining.	
" 25.11.15	Collecting Sick. 5 admitted. 2 Sick evacuated to No. X Veterinary Hospital. 14 remaining. Section marched from Steenvoorde at 11 A.M. to new Billets, arrived 3 P.M.	
Westoutre. 26.11.15	Collecting Sick. Dr. 1 BARRETT. W. No. T28636 Joined Section from Base details. 14 remaining.	
" 27.11.15	Collecting Sick. 3 admitted 17 remaining.	
" 28.11.15	Collecting Sick. 1 admitted 1 destroyed 17 remaining.	
" 29.11.15	Collecting Sick 17 remaining	
" 30.11.15	Collecting Sick. 10 admitted 27 remaining.	

(9 29 6) W4141—463 100,000 9/14 H W V Forms/C. 2118/10

326

11th Moto-Vet. Sec:

Dec

Vol XVII

No. 1

Army Form C. 2118.

Instructions regarding War Diaries and Intelligence Summaries are contained in F. S. Regs., Part II. and the Staff Manual respectively. Title pages will be prepared in manuscript.

WAR DIARY of No. XI Mobile Veterinary Section 3rd Division ~~or~~ ~~INTELLIGENCE~~ ~~SUMMARY~~.

(*Erase heading not required.*)

by E. Lewell Lt. A.V.C. O.C. XI M.V.S.

Hour, Date, Place		Summary of Events and Information	Remarks and references to Appendices
Westoutre	1. 12. 15	Collecting Sick. 30 sick horses admitted. 3 horses reissued cured. 54 horses remaining.	
"	2. 12. 15	Collecting Sick. 6 sick horses admitted. Section marched to Poperinghe & evacuated 50 horses to advanced Veterinary Hospital. 1 horse re-issued cured. 9 horses remaining.	
~~"~~	~~3. 12. 15~~		
"	3. 12. 15	Collecting Sick. 1 horse destroyed. 8 horses remaining.	
"	4. 12. 15	Collecting Sick. 8 horses remaining.	
"	5. 12. 15	Collecting Sick. 1 horse destroyed. 7 remaining.	
"	6. 12. 15	Collecting Sick. 1 horse re-issued cured. 6 horses remaining.	
"	7. 12. 15	Collecting Sick. 3 horses admitted. 1 horse died. 8 horses remaining.	
"	8. 12. 15	Collecting Sick. 19 horses admitted. 27 horses remaining.	
"	9. 12. 15	Collecting Sick. 2 horses admitted. 29 horses remaining. No. 2638 Pte. LUXONA, No. 968 Pte. GIBSON C. H. J.S.E. joined the Section from No. 1 Veterinary Hospital.	
"	10. 12. 15	Collecting Sick. Section marched to Poperinghe & evacuated 23 sick horses to advanced Veterinary Hospital. 6 horses remaining.	
"	11. 12. 15	Collecting Sick. 2 horses admitted. 1 horse died. 7 horses remaining.	

No. 2

Instructions regarding War Diaries and Intelligence Summaries are contained in F. S. Regs., Part II. and the Staff Manual respectively. Title pages will be prepared in manuscript.

WAR DIARY
or
~~INTELLIGENCE SUMMARY~~.
(*Erase heading not required.*)

of No. XI Mobile Veterinary Section 3rd Division by S. Lewell M.A.V.C. O.C. XI M.V.S.

Army Form C. 2118.

Hour, Date, Place	Summary of Events and Information	Remarks and references to Appendices
Westoutre 12. 12. 15.	Collecting Sect. 2 horses admitted. 9 horses remaining	
" 13. 12. 15	Collecting Sect. 1 horse received Cured. 8 horses remaining	
" 14. 12. 15	Collecting Sect. 8 horses remaining.	
" 15. 12. 15	Collecting Sect. 18 horses admitted. 26 horses remaining.	
" 16. 12. 15	Collecting Sect. 2 horses admitted. Section marched to Poperinghe, & evacuated 21 sick to advanced Veterinary Hospital. 7 horses remaining.	
" 17. 12. 15	Collecting Sect. 1 horse admitted. 8 horses remaining.	
" 18. 12. 15	Collecting Sect. 8 remaining.	
" 19. 12. 15.	Collecting Sect. 2 horses admitted. 10 remaining. No 444 Sgt. ROBERTS.C. promoted Staff Sergt. from 1/12/15. Local Corps order 42.	
" 20. 12. 15	Collecting Sect. 1 horse destroyed. 9 remaining. S.E. No. 1173 Sgt. BRADSHAW. R. Joined this Section from No. 19 Veterinary Hospital.	
" 21. 12. 15	Collecting Sect. 1 horse admitted. 10 horses remaining.	
" 22. 12. 15	Collecting Sect. 31 horses admitted. 41 horses remaining	

(9 29 6) W4141—463 100,000 9/14 H W V Forms/C. 2118/10

No. 3.

Instructions regarding War Diaries and Intelligence Summaries are contained in F. S. Regs., Part II. and the Staff Manual respectively. Title pages will be prepared in manuscript.

Army Form C. 2118.

WAR DIARY ~~or INTELLIGENCE~~ SUMMARY.

Of No. XI Mobile Veterinary Section 3rd Division
by E. Sewell. Lt. A.V.C.
OC. XI M.V.S.

(*Erase heading not required.*)

Hour, Date, Place	Summary of Events and Information	Remarks and references to Appendices
Westoutre. 23.12.15.	Collecting Sick. 2 horses admitted. Section marched to Poperinghe & evacuated 24 horses for advanced Veterinary Hospital. 19 remaining. No. 4414 Staff Sergt. Roberts, C. proceeded to No. 8 Veterinary Hospital.	
" 24.12.15	Collecting Sick, 2 horses admitted, 1 horse re-issued cured. 20 horses remaining.	
" 25.12.15	Collecting Sick. 1 horse admitted, 21 horses remaining.	
" 26.12.15	Collecting Sick. 1 horse admitted. 1 horse reissued cured. Section marched to Poperinghe, & evacuated 12 sick to advanced Veterinary Hospital. 9 horses remaining.	
" 27.12.15	Collecting Sick. 1 horse destroyed. 8 horses remaining.	
" 28.12.15	Collecting Sick, 3 horses admitted. 1 horse destroyed. 10 horses remaining.	
" 29.12.15	Collecting Sick, 20 horses admitted. 30 horses remaining.	
" 30.12.15	Collecting Sick. Section marched to Poperinghe & evacuated 21 sick to advanced Veterinary Hospital. 9 remaining.	
" 31.12.15	Collecting Sick, 13 horses admitted. 22 remaining	

3RD DIVISION
DIVL. TROOPS

11TH MOBILE VETY SECTION

JAN - DEC 1916.

3 Dn.

11th Mob. Vet. Sec.

Jan

Vol XVIII

3

No. 1

Army Form C. 2118.

Instructions regarding War Diaries and Intelligence Summaries are contained in F. S. Regs., Part II. and the Staff Manual respectively. Title pages will be prepared in manuscript.

WAR DIARY of No. XI Mobile Veterinary Section 3rd Division. by E. Sewell A.V.C. O.C. XI M.V.S.
or
~~INTELLIGENCE SUMMARY.~~
(Erase heading not required.)

Hour, Date, Place	Summary of Events and Information	Remarks and references to Appendices
A1. Westoutre. 1.1.16.	Collecting Sick. 2 horses admitted, 9 evacuated from Poperinghe, 15 remaining.	
" 2.1.16	Collecting Sick. 4 horses admitted, 3 re-issued cured, 16 remaining.	
" 3.1.16	Collecting Sick. 4 horses admitted, 20 remaining.	
" 4.1.16	Collecting Sick. 1 horse admitted, 21 remaining.	
" 5.1.16	Collecting Sick. 24 horses admitted, 1 re-issued cured 44 horses remaining.	
" 6.1.16	Collecting Sick. 2 horses admitted, 36 evacuated from Poperinghe, 1 destroyed, 9 remaining	
" 7.1.16	Collecting Sick. 1 horse admitted. 10 horses remaining.	
" 8.1.16	Collecting Sick. 3 horses admitted, 13 remaining.	
" 9.1.16	Collecting Sick. 43 horses admitted, 56 remaining.	
" 10.1.16	Collecting Sick. 1 horse admitted, 1 destroyed, 43 evacuated from Poperinghe 13 remaining.	
" 11.1.16	Collecting Sick. 3 horses admitted, 16 remaining.	
" 12.1.16	Collecting Sick. 29 horses admitted 45 remaining	
" 13.1.16	Collecting Sick 3 horses admitted, Section marched to Poperinghe & entrained 34 sick horses for Advanced Veterinary Hospital	
"	14 horses remaining	
" 14.1.16	Collecting Sick. 2 horses admitted, 16 remaining.	
" 15.1.16	Collecting Sick 17 horses admitted, 2 re-issued cured 1 died 30 remaining.	
" 16.1.16	Collecting Sick. 4 horses admitted, & Section marched to Poperinghe & entrained 23 sick horses for No. 13 Veterinary Hospital. 1 horse destroyed. 10 horses remaining. The Section was inspected by the 5th Corps Commander. Lt. General H. D. Fanshawe C.B.	

Instructions regarding War Diaries and Intelligence Summaries are contained in F. S. Regs., Part II. and the Staff Manual respectively. Title pages will be prepared in manuscript.

WAR DIARY No 2

~~or~~

~~INTELLIGENCE SUMMARY.~~

(*Erase heading not required.*)

of No. XI Mobile Veterinary Section 3rd Division by E. Sewell Lt. A. V. C. O. C. XI M. V. S.

Army Form C. 2118.

Hour, Date, Place	Summary of Events and Information	Remarks and references to Appendices
Westoutre 17. 1. 16	Collecting Sick, 4 horses admitted, 14 remaining	
" 18. 1. 16	Collecting Sick. 4 horses admitted, 18 remaining.	
" 19. 1. 16	Collecting Sick. 39 horses admitted, 57 remaining.	
" 20. 1. 16	Collecting Sick 3 horses admitted 1 died 1 destroyed, 4 re-issued Cured. Section marched to Poperinghe & entrained 39 Sick horses for No. 13 Veterinary Hospital. 15 horses remaining	
" 21. 1. 16	Collecting Sick. 3 horses admitted, 6 re-issued Cured, 12 remaining.	
" 22. 1. 16	Collecting Sick 1 horse admitted, 13 horses remaining.	
" 23. 1. 16	Collecting Sick 18 horses admitted 31 remaining.	
" 24. 1. 16	Collecting Sick. 4 horses admitted 1 re-issued cured, Section marched to Poperinghe & entrained 26 Sick to No. 13 Veterinary Hospital. 8 horses remaining.	
" 25. 1. 16	Collecting Sick, 20 horses admitted, 28 remaining.	
" 26. 1. 16	Collecting Sick. 48 horses admitted. 76 horses remaining.	
" 27. 1. 16	Collecting Sick 19 horses admitted 1 re-issued Cured. Section marched to Poperinghe & entrained 14 Cost & 66 Sick horses to No. 13 Veterinary Hospital	
" 28 1. 16	Collecting Sick, 3 admitted, 6 evacuated to No. 13 Veterinary Hospital 11 remaining	
" 29. 1. 16	Collecting Sick. 10 horses admitted. 21 remaining	
" 30. 1. 16	Collecting Sick 12 horses admitted, 2 re-issued Cured. 31 remaining.	
" 31. 1. 16	Collecting Sick 10 horses admitted, Section marched to Poperinghe & entrained 23 Sick horses for No. 13 Veterinary Hospital 18 horses remaining	

3

11 Mobile Vety Sec

Feb

Vol XIX

No. 1

Army Form C. 2118.

Instructions regarding War Diaries and Intelligence Summaries are contained in F. S. Regs., Part II. and the Staff Manual respectively. Title pages will be prepared in manuscript.

WAR DIARY
~~or~~ of XI Mobile Veterinary Section 3rd Division

~~INTELLIGENCE~~ SUMMARY.

(*Erase heading not required.*)

by E Sewell Capt. A.V.C.

Hour, Date, Place	Summary of Events and Information	Remarks and references to Appendices
1.2.16 Westoutre.	Collecting Sick. 8 admitted, 1 destroyed, 25 sick remaining	
2.2.16 "	Collecting Sick. 28 sick admitted, 4 re-issued cured 49 remaining.	
3.2.16 "	Collecting Sick. 5 sick admitted, 1 destroyed, 1 re-issued cured. Section marched to Poperinghe & entrained 34 sick horses for No. 13 Veterinary Hospital. 18 remaining	
4.2.16 "	Collecting Sick. 10 sick admitted, 9 re-issued cured, 19 remaining.	
5.2.16 "	Collecting Sick. 6 sick admitted, 25 remaining	
6.2.16 "	Collecting Sick. 16 sick admitted, 2 re-issued, 39 remaining	
7.2.16 "	Collecting Sick, 2 admitted, 1 died. Section marched to Poperinghe & evacuated 32 sick to No. 13 Veterinary Hospital. 8 remaining	
8.2.16 "	Collecting Sick. 8 sick admitted, 16 remaining	
9.2.16 "	Collecting Sick. 14 admitted, 30 remaining	

(9 29 6) W4141—463 100,000 9/14 H W V Forms/C. 2118/10

No. 2

Army Form C. 2118.

Instructions regarding War Diaries and Intelligence Summaries are contained in F. S. Regs., Part II. and the Staff Manual respectively. Title pages will be prepared in manuscript.

WAR DIARY
or
~~INTELLIGENCE~~ SUMMARY.

of No. XI Mobile Veterinary Section 3rd Division by E. Lloyd Capt. A.V.C.

(*Erase heading not required.*)

Hour, Date, Place	Summary of Events and Information	Remarks and references to Appendices
10.2.16 Westoutre	Collecting Sick 1 admitted. Section marched to Poperinghe & entrained 25 sick for No. 13 Veterinary Hospital. 6 remaining.	
11.2.16 "	Collecting Sick. 2 sick admitted 8 remaining	
12.2.16 WEMAERS-CAPPEL	Section marched from Westoutre at 9 a.m. via Steenvoorde & arrived at billet WEMAERS-CAPPEL at 4 P.M. 3 sick horses were handed over to No. 29 Mobile Veterinary Section. 5 remaining	
13.2.16 NORDAUSQUES	Section marched from WEMAERS-CAPPEL at 9 A.M. via WATTEN, & arrived at billet NORDAUSQUES, at 3:30 P.M. 5 remaining.	
14.2.16 "	Collecting Sick, 2 sick returned cured, 3 remaining.	
15.2.16 "	Collecting Sick 3 remaining.	
16.2.16 "	Collecting Sick 4 admitted. 7 remaining	
17.2.16 "	Collecting Sick. 2 admitted 9 remaining.	
18.2.16 "	Collecting Sick. 1 admitted. 1 destroyed, 9 remaining	
19.2.16 "	Collecting Sick 6 admitted. 15 remaining	

(9 29 6) W4141—463 100,000 9/14 H W V Forms/C. 2118/10

No. 3

Instructions regarding War Diaries and Intelligence Summaries are contained in F. S. Regs., Part II. and the Staff Manual respectively. Title pages will be prepared in manuscript.

WAR DIARY
or
~~INTELLIGENCE~~ SUMMARY.
of No. 8 Mobile Veterinary Section 3rd Division by E. Sewell Capt. A.V.C.

(Erase heading not required.)

Army Form C. 2118.

Hour, Date, Place	Summary of Events and Information	Remarks and references to Appendices
20.2.16 Nordausques	Collecting Sick. 14 admitted 1 returned cured 28 remaining. No. 564 Corp. KNIGHT J. was awarded 60 days No. 2 Field Punishment & reduced to the ranks, by a Field General Court Martial held at Hdqs of Cheshire Field Co. R.E. at MONNECOVE, for "wilful defiance of a lawful command given personally by a superior officer". The award was confirmed by G.O.C. 3rd Division & duly promulgated.	
21.2.16 "	Collecting Sick. 2 admitted, 1 destroyed, 1 returned cured, 28 remaining.	
22.2.16 "	Collecting Sick 2 admitted. 30 remaining.	
23.2.16 "	Collecting Sick. 13 admitted. Section marched to WATTEN & evacuated 30 sick to No. 13 Veterinary Hospital. 13 remaining.	
24.2.16 "	Collecting Sick 8 admitted. 21 remaining	
25.2.16 "	Collecting Sick. 5 admitted. Section marched to Watten & evacuated 14 sick to No. 13 Veterinary Hospital. 1 returned cured. 11 remaining	

(9 29 6) W 4141—463 100,000 9/14 H W V Forms/C. 2118/10

No. 4

Instructions regarding War Diaries and Intelligence Summaries are contained in F. S. Regs., Part II. and the Staff Manual respectively. Title pages will be prepared in manuscript.

WAR DIARY

~~or~~ of No. XI Mobile Veterinary Section 3rd Division by E. Sewell Capt. A.V.C.

~~INTELLIGENCE~~ SUMMARY.

(Erase heading not required.)

Army Form C. 2118.

Hour, Date, Place	Summary of Events and Information	Remarks and references to Appendices
26.2.16 Nordausques.	Collecting Sick. 7 admitted. 18 remaining	
27.2.16 "	Collecting Sick. 12 Sick admitted. 2 destroyed 28 remaining.	
28.2.16 "	Collecting Sick. 21 Sick admitted. 1 destroyed 3 rejoined unit 45 remaining	
29.2.16 "	Collecting Sick 3 admitted. Section marched to WATTEN & evacuated 38 Sick to No. 13 Veterinary Hospital. 10 remaining.	

(9 29 6) W4141—463 100,000 9/14 H W V Forms/C. 2118/10

3

11 Mob Vety Sec

Vol XX

No. 1.

Army Form C. 2118.

Instructions regarding War Diaries and Intelligence Summaries are contained in F. S. Regs., Part II. and the Staff Manual respectively. Title pages will be prepared in manuscript.

WAR DIARY of No. XI Mobile Veterinary Section by E Sewell Capt. A.V.C.

or

~~INTELLIGENCE SUMMARY.~~

(*Erase heading not required.*)

Hour, Date, Place	Summary of Events and Information	Remarks and references to Appendices
Nordausques 1. 3. 16.	Collecting Sick. 3 admitted, 1 destroyed. 12 sick remaining.	
" 2. 3. 16.	Collecting Sick. 4 admitted, 1 destroyed, 15 sick remaining	
" 3. 3. 16	Collecting Sick. 5 admitted, 1 destroyed, 19 remaining.	
" 4. 3. 16	Collecting Sick. 9 admitted, 4 reissued cured, 24 remaining.	
" 5. 3. 16	Collecting Sick. 17 admitted. 41 remaining. Section marched to WATTEN & entrained	
" 6. 3. 16	Collecting Sick. 2 admitted Section marched Hospital. 10 remaining. 33 sick to No 13 Veterinary	
" 7. 3. 16	Collecting Sick. 2 admitted, 12 remaining.	
" 8. 3. 16	Collecting Sick. 1 admitted, 13 remaining.	
" 9. 3. 16	Collecting Sick. 4 admitted, 17 remaining.	
" 10. 3. 16	Collecting Sick. 1 admitted, 1 died. Section marched to Audruicq & entrained 10 sick horses to No. 13 Veterinary Hospital. 7 remaining	
Wemaers Cappel 11. 3. 16	Section marched from Nordausques at 9 A.M. via Watten, & billeted at Wemaers-Cappel at 2 P.M. 7 remaining.	
Westoutre 12. 3. 16	Section marched from Wemaers-Cappel & arrived at billet at Westoutre at 1.30 P.M. 2 sick admitted, 9 remaining. S.E. 10577 Corp. STOKES W. joined section from No 19 Veterinary Hospital.	
" 13. 3. 16	Collecting Sick. 7 admitted, 1 reissued cured, 15 remaining	
" 14. 3. 16	Collecting Sick, 15 remaining.	
" 15. 3. 16	Collecting Sick 15 admitted 1 reissued cured 29 remaining	
" 16. 3. 16	Collecting Sick, 48 admitted, 2 destroyed, 75 remaining	

No. 2

Instructions regarding War Diaries and Intelligence Summaries are contained in F. S. Regs., Part II. and the Staff Manual respectively. Title pages will be prepared in manuscript.

WAR DIARY of No 11 Mobile Veterinary Section 3rd Division by E Sewell Capt. A.V.C.

or

~~**INTELLIGENCE SUMMARY.**~~

(Erase heading not required.)

Army Form C. 2118.

Hour, Date, Place		Summary of Events and Information	Remarks and references to Appendices
Westoutre	17. 3. 16	Collecting Sick 1 admitted Section marched to Poperinghe & entrained 62 sick to No. 13 Veterinary Hospital. 2 re-issued cured, 2 remaining.	
"	18. 3. 16	Collecting Sick 10 admitted. 1 destroyed, 21 remaining.	
"	19. 3. 16	Collecting Sick. 1 admitted. No 968 Pte GIBSON C. admitted to Hospital & evacuated. 22 remaining	
"	20. 3. 16	Collecting Sick. 1 admitted, 2 reissued cured, 21 remaining	
"	21. 3. 16	Collecting Sick. 2 admitted, 23 remaining	
"	22. 3. 16	Collecting Sick, 31 admitted, 2 destroyed, 4 reissued, 48 remaining	
"	23. 3. 16	Collecting Sick. 3 admitted Section marched to Poperinghe & entrained 35 sick to No. 13 Veterinary Hospital. 7 reissued cured 9 remaining.	
"	24. 3. 16	Collecting Sick. 9 remaining	
"	25. 3. 16	Collecting Sick, 1 admitted, 1 reissued 9 remaining	
"	26. 3. 16	Collecting Sick 8 admitted 1 destroyed No. 2398 Sgt. EVEREST. A. ~~joined~~ attached to Section from 131 Bde R.F.A. for a months training. 16 remaining	

(9 29 6) W4141—463 100,000 9/14 H W V Forms/C. 2118/10

Instructions regarding War Diaries and Intelligence Summaries are contained in F. S. Regs., Part II. and the Staff Manual respectively. Title pages will be prepared in manuscript.

Army Form C. 2118.

WAR DIARY of No. 3 Mobile Veterinary Section 3rd Division
~~or INTELLIGENCE SUMMARY.~~ by E Sewell Capt. A.V.C.

(Erase heading not required.)

Hour, Date, Place		Summary of Events and Information	Remarks and references to Appendices
Westoutre	27. 3. 16	Collecting Sick 5 admitted Section marched to Poperinghe & entrained 10 sick to No. 13 Veterinary Hospital. 11 remaining.	
"	28. 3. 16	Collecting Sick 11 remaining.	
"	29. 3. 16	Collecting Sick 21 admitted, 3 received cured 25 remaining.	
"	30. 3. 16	Collecting Sick, 5 admitted. 1 died. Section marched to Poperinghe & evacuated 23 sick to No. 13 Veterinary Hospital. 9 remaining.	
"	31. 3. 16	Collecting Sick. 4 admitted, 2 destroyed 11 remaining	

(9 29 6) W 4141—463 100,000 9/14 H W V Forms/C. 2118/10

3

11 Mob Vety Sect

Vol XXI

Army Form C. 2118.

No. 1 WAR DIARY of No. XI Mobile Veterinary Section 3rd Division. ~~or INTELLIGENCE~~ SUMMARY

(Erase heading not required.)

by E. Sewell Capt. A.V.C. O.C. XI M.V.S.

Instructions regarding War Diaries and Intelligence Summaries are contained in F. S. Regs., Part II. and the Staff Manual respectively. Title Pages will be prepared in manuscript.

Place	Date	Hour	Summary of Events and Information	Remarks and references to Appendices
Westoutre	1.4.16		Collecting Sick, 11 sick remaining. Nos. 2132 Pte WATSON. A, 1280 Pte. WHEELER. E, 6130 Pte. MILES. H. Joined the Section from No. 2 Veterinary Hospital.	
"	~~do~~			
"	2.4.16		Collecting Sick, 34 admitted, 45 remaining.	
"	3.4.16		Collecting Sick, Section marched to Poperinghe & entrained 42 horses for No. 13 Veterinary Hospital, 6 remaining. Nos. 3017 Pte JUDD. J, 1960 Pte. CLISSOLD. H, 5075 Pte. TINSON. W. left the Section & proceeded to No. 2 Veterinary Hospital Havre.	
	4.4.16		Collecting Sick, 2 admitted, 8 remaining.	
	5.4.16		Collecting Sick, 12 admitted, 2 destroyed, 18 remaining.	
	6.4.16		Collecting Sick, 5 admitted, Section marched to Poperinghe & entrained 11 sick for No. 13 Veterinary Hospital, 12 remaining.	
	7.4.16		Collecting Sick, 1 admitted. Section marched to Poperinghe & entrained 5 sick for No. 13 Veterinary Hospital. 8 remaining. Section marched from Westoutre at 10:30 A.M. & arrived at new Billet at Coq de Paille at 1 P.M.	

Instructions regarding War Diaries and Intelligence Summaries are contained in F. S. Regs., Part II. and the Staff Manual respectively. Title Pages will be prepared in manuscript.

Army Form C. 2118.

No. 2.

WAR DIARY of No. XI Mobile Veterinary Section 33rd Division by C. Sewell Capt. A.V.C. O.C. XI M.V.S.
or
~~INTELLIGENCE SUMMARY~~
(Erase heading not required.)

Place	Date	Hour	Summary of Events and Information	Remarks and references to Appendices
Flêtre	8.4.16		Collecting Sick 8 remaining.	
"	9.4.16		Collecting Sick, 4 admitted. 12 remaining	
"	10.4.16		Collecting Sick 9 admitted. 21 remaining.	
"	11.4.16		Collecting Sick. 3 admitted. Section marched to Godewaersvelde & evacuated 12 Sick to No. 13 Veterinary Hospital, 12 remaining	
"	12.4.16		Collecting Sick. 3 admitted 15 remaining.	
"	13.4.16		Collecting Sick. 5 admitted. 2 Reissued Cured. 18 remaining.	
"	14.4.16		Collecting Sick. 2 admitted. 1 Died. 1 reissued cured 18 remaining. Section was inspected by A.D.V.S. 33rd Division.	
"	15.4.16		Collecting Sick. 3 admitted. 1 reissued cured. Section marched to Caestre & entrained 7 Sick to No. 13 Veterinary Hospital. 13 remaining.	
"	16.4.16		Collecting Sick. 28 admitted 41 remaining.	
"	17.4.16		Collecting Sick. 1 admitted. 31 Sick entrained at Bailleul for No. 13 Veterinary Hospital, 11 remaining.	
"	18.4.16		Collecting Sick. 4 admitted. 15 remaining.	
"	19.4.16		Collecting Sick. 9 admitted 24 remaining	
"	20.4.16.		Collecting Sick. 18 admitted. 2 reissued. 40 remaining. No. 7053 S/S POWELL ~~joined section for~~ M.G. Co. 76th Bde., + No. 15769 S.S. WILLIAMS. R. R.W.F. 76th Bde. Joined Section for 14 days instruction.	

2449 Wt. W14957/M90 750,000 1/16 J.B.C. & A. Forms/C.2118/12.

Instructions regarding War Diaries and Intelligence Summaries are contained in F. S. Regs., Part II. and the Staff Manual respectively. Title Pages will be prepared in manuscript.

No. 3

Army Form C. 2118.

WAR DIARY of No. XI Mobile Veterinary Section 3rd Division

or

~~INTELLIGENCE SUMMARY~~

(Erase heading not required.)

by E. Lewell Capt. A.V.C. O.C. XI M.V.S.

Place	Date	Hour	Summary of Events and Information	Remarks and references to Appendices
Zelobes	21.4.16		Collecting Sick. 3 admitted. 1 reissued Cured. 1 died. 25 Sick entrained at Bailleul for No. 13 Veterinary Hospital. 11 remaining. No. 564 Pte KNIGHT, J. proceeded to No. 19 Veterinary Hospital Rouen on expiration of Sentence.	
"	22.4.16		Collecting Sick. 22 admitted. 1 reissued Cured. 37 remaining.	
"	23.4.16		Collecting Sick. 19 admitted. 2 reissued Cured. 54 remaining.	
"	24.4.16		Collecting Sick. 6 admitted. 40 Sick entrained at Godwaersvelde for No. 13 Veterinary Hospital. 20 remaining.	
"	25.4.16		Collecting Sick. 4 admitted. 24 remaining.	
"	26.4.16		Collecting Sick. 9 admitted. 3 reissued Cured. 30 remaining.	
"	27.4.16		Collecting Sick. 2 admitted. 1 destroyed. 1 reissued Cured. 30 remaining.	
"	28.4.16		Collecting Sick. 3 reissued Cured. 19 Sick entrained at Godwaersvelde for No. 13 Veterinary Hospital. 8 remaining.	
"	29.4.16		Collecting Sick. 2 admitted. 10 remaining.	
"	30.4.16.		Collecting Sick. 2 admitted. 1 Sick horse reissued Cured. 11 remaining. Section marched from Zelobes at 9.30 A.M. & arrived at new Billet at Westoutre at 12 A.M.	

2449 Wt. W14957/M90 750,000 1/16 J.B.C. & A. Forms/C.2118/12.

No 1.

WAR DIARY of No. ~~XI~~ XI Mobile Veterinary Section 3rd Division

~~or~~

~~**INTELLIGENCE SUMMARY**~~

(Erase heading not required.)

by E. Atwell Capt. A.V.C.

Army Form C. 2118. 3

Instructions regarding War Diaries and Intelligence Summaries are contained in F. S. Regs., Part II. and the Staff Manual respectively. Title Pages will be prepared in manuscript.

Vol 22

Place	Date	Hour	Summary of Events and Information	Remarks and references to Appendices
Westoutre	1.5.16		Collecting sick. 1 admitted. 12 sick remaining.	
"	2.5.16		Collecting sick. 2 admitted. 14 remaining.	
"	3.5.16		Collecting sick. 16 admitted. 3 issued cured. 27 remaining.	
"	4.5.16		Collecting sick. Section marched to Bailleul & evacuated 16 horses to No. 13 Veterinary Hospital. 3 issued cured. 8 remaining.	
"	5.5.16		Collecting sick. 2 admitted. 10 sick remaining.	
"	6.5.16		Collecting sick. 1 admitted. 11 remaining.	
"	7.5.16		Collecting sick. 3 admitted, 1 issued cured. 13 remaining. S.E No. 2398 Sgt. EVEREST. W. at his own request reverted to Private. Pte proceeded to	
"			No. 2 Veterinary Hospital, on this date.	
"	8.5.16		Collecting sick. 9 admitted 22 sick remaining.	
"	9.5.16		Collecting sick. Section marched to Bailleul & entrained 14 sick to No. 13 Veterinary Hospital. 8 remaining.	
"	10.5.16		Collecting sick. 4 admitted. 12 remaining. Section marched to Scherpenberg Range, & went through a Course of Musketry.	
"	11.5.16		Collecting sick. 16 admitted. 28 remaining.	
"	12.5.16		Collecting sick. 2 admitted. 15 sick entrained at Bailleul for No. 13 Veterinary Hospital. 15 remaining.	
"	13.5.16		Collecting sick. 1 admitted. 16 remaining.	
"	14.5.16		Collecting sick. 3 admitted. 2 issued cured. 17 remaining.	
"	15.5.16		Collecting sick. 10 admitted. 27 remaining. S.E No. 2132 Pte. WATSON. A. promoted to rank of Sgt. & posted to 71st Infantry Brigade.	

2449 Wt. W14957/M90 750,000 1/16 J.B.C. & A. Forms/C.2118/12.

Army Form C. 2118.

Instructions regarding War Diaries and Intelligence Summaries are contained in F. S. Regs., Part II. and the Staff Manual respectively. Title Pages will be prepared in manuscript.

No. 2 WAR DIARY of No. 21 Mobile Veterinary Section 37th Division

~~or INTELLIGENCE~~ SUMMARY

(*Erase heading not required.*)

by E. Lee Capt. A.V.C.

Place	Date	Hour	Summary of Events and Information	Remarks and references to Appendices
Westoutre	16.5.16		Collecting Sick. Section marched to Bailleul & entrained 11 sick for No. 13 Veterinary Hospital. 16 remaining.	
"	17.5.16		Collecting Sick. 1 reissued Cured. 15 remaining.	
"	18.5.16		Collecting Sick. 5 admitted 4 reissued Cured. 16 remaining	
"	19.5.16		Collecting Sick. 3 admitted. Section marched to Bailleul & entrained 8 sick for No. 13 Veterinary Hospital. 11 remaining.	
"	20.5.16		Collecting Sick. 3 admitted. 14 remaining.	
"	21.5.16		Collecting Sick. 1 admitted 1 reissued Cured, 14 remaining.	
"	22.5.16		Collecting Sick. 5 admitted. 1 reissued Cured. 18 remaining.	
"	23.5.16		Collecting Sick. Section marched to Bailleul & entrained 6 sick for No. 13 Veterinary Hospital. 3 reissued Cured. 9 remaining.	
"	24.5.16		Collecting Sick. 3 reissued. 6 remaining.	
"	25.5.16		Collecting Sick. 6 admitted. 12 remaining.	
"	26.5.16		Collecting Sick. 4 admitted. 7 sick entrained at Bailleul for No. 13 Veterinary Hospital 2 reissued. ~~7 remaining~~	
"	27.5.16		Collecting Sick. 1 reissued Cured 6 remaining.	
"	28.5.16		Collecting Sick. 2 admitted 1 reissued Cured 7 remaining	
"	29.5.16		Collecting Sick. 9 admitted. 16 remaining	
"	30.5.16		Collecting Sick. 5 admitted. 14 sick entrained at Bailleul for No. 13 Veterinary Hospital. Section marched to New Billets at Coq de Paille arriving 12 A.M. 7 remaining.	
Coq de Paille	31.5.16		Collecting Sick. 8 admitted 2 reissued Cured. 13 remaining. Nos 7055 L/c POWELL A., & 15169 S.S. WILLIAMS R. rejoined their units on completion of training.	

2449 Wt. W14957/M90 750,000 1/16 J.B.C. & A. Forms/C.2118/12.

No. 1.

WAR DIARY
or ~~INTELLIGENCE SUMMARY~~
of No. XI Mobile Veterinary Section 3rd Division

(Erase heading not required.)

by E Sewell Capt. A.V.C.

XI Mob Vety Sec

Army Form C. 2118.

3

Instructions regarding War Diaries and Intelligence Summaries are contained in F. S. Regs., Part II. and the Staff Manual respectively. Title Pages will be prepared in manuscript.

Place	Date	Hour	Summary of Events and Information	Remarks and references to Appendices
Cog de Paille	1.6.16		Collecting Sick. 11 admitted. 4 issued cured. No 834 Pte BENNETT W. Joined the Section from No. 12 Veterinary Hospital. 20 Sick remaining.	Vol 23
"	2.6.16		Collecting Sick. 4 admitted. Section marched to Caestre & entrained 16 Sick to No 13 Veterinary Hospital. 8 remaining.	
"	3.6.16.		Collecting Sick. 8 admitted. 16 remaining.	
"	4.6.16		Collecting Sick. 3 admitted. 2 issued cured. 17 remaining.	
"	5.6.16.		Collecting Sick. 12 admitted. 29 remaining.	
"	6.6.16.		Collecting Sick. 20 admitted. Section marched to Caestre & entrained 23 Sick for No. 13 Veterinary Hospital. No. 13682 Pte KENNY T. Joined Section from A.D.V.S. 3rd Division. 26 remaining.	
"	7.6.16.		Collecting Sick. 7 admitted. 2 issued cured. 31 remaining.	
"	8.6.16.		Collecting Sick. 10 admitted. 41 remaining.	
"	9.6.16		Collecting Sick. 7 admitted. Section marched to Caestre & entrained 24 Sick for No. 13 Veterinary Hospital. 1 issued. 23 remaining.	
"	10.6.16		Collecting Sick. 1 admitted. 1 issued. No. T4-059792 Dr. NASH C., A.S.C. Joined Section from No. 1 Base Transport Depot. 23 remaining.	
"	11.6.16.		Collecting Sick. 3 issued 20 remaining.	
"	12.6.16		Collecting Sick. 13 admitted 1 Died. 32 remaining.	
"	13.6.16		Collecting Sick 3 admitted. Section marched to Caestre & entrained 20 Sick for No. 13 Veterinary Hospital. 15 remaining.	
"	14.6.16.		Collecting Sick. 2 admitted. 1 issued. 16 remaining.	
"	15.6.16		Collecting Sick. 8 admitted. 4 issued. 20 remaining.	
"	16.6.16		Collecting Sick. 5 admitted. Section marched to Caestre & entrained 8 Sick for No. 13 Veterinary Hospital. 17 remaining.	

2449 Wt. W14957/M90 750,000 1/16 J.B.C. & A. Forms/C.2118/12.

Instructions regarding War Diaries and Intelligence Summaries are contained in F. S. Regs., Part II. and the Staff Manual respectively. Title Pages will be prepared in manuscript.

Army Form C. 2118.

WAR DIARY No. 2
or
~~INTELLIGENCE SUMMARY~~
of No. 31 Mobile Veterinary Section 3rd Division by E. Sewell Capt. A.V.C.

(Erase heading not required.)

Place	Date	Hour	Summary of Events and Information	Remarks and references to Appendices
Cogde Paille		17.6.16	Collecting Sect. 6 admitted 1 issued 22 remaining.	
"		18.6.16	Collecting Sect. Section marched from Cogde Paille at 7:30 A.M. arrived & billeted at WEMAERS-CAPPEL at 1:15 P.M. 1 destroyed 21 remaining.	
Wemaers Cappel		19.6.16	Section marched from WEMAERS-CAPPEL at 7:30 A.M. arrived BROXEELE at 11:15 A.M. 21 remaining.	
Broxeele		20.6.16	Section marched from BROXEELE at 8 A.M. arrived TILQUES 1 P.M. 5 sick evacuated to No. 13 Veterinary Hospital, & 5 evacuated to No. 23 Veterinary Hospital. 3 admitted 14 remaining.	
TILQUES		21.6.16	Collecting Sect. 6 admitted 11 evacuated 2 issued. 7 remaining. Section was inspected by Brig. General J. Moore & Col. Nuttall.	
"		22.6.16	Collecting Sect. 9 admitted. 6 issued. No. 6130 Pte. MILLS A. proceeded to No. 2 Veterinary Hospital. 9 remaining.	
"		23.6.16	Collecting Sect. 9 admitted 11 evacuated 7 remaining.	
"		24.6.16	Collecting Sect. 3 admitted. 10 remaining.	
"		25.6.16	Collecting Sect. 2 admitted. 6 evacuated 1 issued. 5 remaining	
"		26.6.16	Collecting Sect. 8 admitted. 13 remaining.	
"		27.6.16	Collecting Sect. 9 admitted. 7 evacuated. 1 issued. 13 remaining.	
"		28.6.16	Collecting Sect. 3 admitted. 3 issued. 6 evacuated. 7 remaining.	
"		29.6.16	Collecting Sect. 4 admitted 2 issued. 9 remaining.	
"		30.6.16	Collecting Sect. 10 admitted 7 evacuated. 1 issued. 11 remaining.	

2449 Wt. W14957/M90 750,000 1/16 J.B.C. & A. Forms/C.2118/12.

A. D. V. S.
3rd Division

Herewith War Diary of No. XI M. V. S.
for July 1916.

3. 8. 16

E Sewell
Capt. A.V.C.
O.C. XI M.V.S.

3rd Divn Q

Forwarded

G Conder
Major
ADVS 3 Div

3. 8. 16

Instructions regarding War Diaries and Intelligence Summaries are contained in F. S. Regs., Part II. and the Staff Manual respectively. Title Pages will be prepared in manuscript.

WAR DIARY No. 1.
or
INTELLIGENCE SUMMARY
(Erase heading not required.)

of No. XI Mobile Veterinary Section 3rd Division by C. Atwell Capt. A.V.C.

Army Form C. 2118.

Vol 24

Place	Date	Hour	Summary of Events and Information	Remarks and references to Appendices
TILQUES	1.7.16		8 sick evacuated to No. 23 Vety. Hospital ST. OMER. Section marched from TILQUES	
LANCHES	2.7.16		at 6 P.M. & entrained at WIZERNES at 8:12 P.M.	
BETTINCOURT	3.7.16		Section detrained CANDAS 9 A.M. & marched to billets at LANCHES arriving 2 P.M.	
			Section marched from LANCHES 4:30 P.M. & billeted BETTINCOURT 6.30 P.M. 5 Miles.	
"	4.7.16	9 P.M.	Section marched from BETTINCOURT	
BERTANGLES	5.7.16	3:15 A.M.	arrived. 9 Miles	
"	5.7.16.	10 P.M.	Section marched from BERTANGLES.	
LAHOUSSYE	6.7.16	3:20 A.M.	arrived. 8 Miles	
"	6.7.16	12:30 P.M.	Section marched from BAV LAHOUSSYE.	
BOIS-de-TAILLE	6.7.16	3 P.M.	arrived. 8 Miles	
BOIS-de-TAILLE.	7.7.16	5 P.M.	Section marched from BOIS-de-TAILLE	
SAILLY-LE-SEC	7.7.16	6 P.M.	arrived 3 Miles	
"	8.7.16		No. 497 Corp. LAWS. J. admitted to Hospital & evacuated. Collecting Station posted in BOIS-de-TAILLE	
"	9.7.16			
"	10.7.16		Collecting Station posted at GROVETOWN Advanced Dressing Station posted at BILLON FARM.	
"	11.7.16	→	18 sick evacuated to No. 7 Vety. Hospital FORGES-LES-EAUX.	
"	12.7.16		A Considerable number of wounded horses were dressed at advanced Dressing Station,	
"	13.7.16			
"	14.7.16			
"	15.7.16	3 P.M.	Section marched from SAILLY-LE-SEC	
GROVETOWN	15.7.16	5 P.M.	arrived. 6 Miles	

2449 Wt. W14957/M90 750,000 1/16 J.B.C. & A. Forms/C.2118/12.

Instructions regarding War Diaries and Intelligence Summaries are contained in F. S. Regs., Part II. and the Staff Manual respectively. Title Pages will be prepared in manuscript.

WAR DIARY No. 2 of No. XI M.V.S. 3rd Division
or
INTELLIGENCE SUMMARY
(Erase heading not required.)

by Elwell Capt. A.V.C.

Army Form C. 2118.

Place	Date	Hour	Summary of Events and Information	Remarks and references to Appendices
GROVETOWN	16.7.16		22 Sick horses evacuated from MERICOURT to No. 7 Vety. Hospital FORGES-LES-EAUX.	
"	17.7.16			
"	18.7.16		34 Sick evacuated from MERICOURT to No. 7 Vety. Hospital FORGES-LES-EAUX.	
"	19.7.16			
"	20.7.16		20 Sick evacuated to No. 7 Vety. Hospital FORGES-LES-EAUX from MERICOURT.	
"	21.7.16			
"	22.7.16		35 Sick evacuated from MERICOURT to No. 7 Vety. Hospital.	
"	23.7.16			
"	24.7.16	8:30AM	30 Sick evacuated from MERICOURT to No. 7 Vety. Hospital.	
	"	8:30AM	Advanced Dressing Station moved towards BRONFAY FARM, owing to Shell fire.	
	"	5:30PM	Advanced Dressing Station moved BRAY side of BRONFAY FARM owing to Shell fire.	
"	25.7.16			
"	26.7.16		33 Sick evacuated from MERICOURT to No 7 Vety. Hospital. Advanced Dressing Station withdrawn	
"	27.7.16			
"	28.7.16	9:30AM	Section marched from GROVETOWN.	
VILLE-SUR-ANCRE	"	11:30AM	21 Sick evacuated at MERICOURT for No. 7 Vety. Hospital.	
		12:30PM	Section arrived Billet 4 Miles	
"	29.7.16			
"	30.7.16		21 Sick evacuated from MERICOURT for No. 7 Vety. Hospital.	
"	31.7.16		6 Sick evacuated for No. 7 Vety. Hospital. No. 1349 Pte. ROOKS? joined Section from No. 1 Vety. Hospital	

No. 1

WAR DIARY of No. XI Mobile Veterinary Section 3rd Division

or

INTELLIGENCE SUMMARY

(Erase heading not required.)

by E. Sewell Capt. A.V.C.

Army Form C. 2118.

Instructions regarding War Diaries and Intelligence Summaries are contained in F. S. Regs., Part II. and the Staff Manual respectively. Title Pages will be prepared in manuscript.

Vol 25

Place	Date	Hour	Summary of Events and Information	Remarks and references to Appendices
VILLE-SUR-ANCRE	1.8.16		Nothing to record	
"	2.8.16		Collecting Station withdrawn from GROVETOWN.	
"	3.8.16		20 sick horses evacuated from MERICOURT to No. 7 Vety. Hospital.	
"	4.8.16		No. 3284 Pte. BELCHER.C. put under arrest for sleeping on his Post.	
"	5.8.16		A.V. Corps Orders No. 326 received sanctioning the transfer of No. 3284 Pte. BELCHER C. to 12th Batn. Royal Fusiliers. In consequence I applied to G.O.C. 3rd Division for permission to deal with No. 3284 Pte. BELCHER C. summarily.	
"	6.8.16		53 sick horses evacuated from MERICOURT to No. 7 Vety. Hospital.	
"	7.8.16		Nothing to record.	
"	8.8.16		No. 3284 Pte. BELCHER.C. proceeded to 12th Batn. Royal Fusiliers, transferred vide A.V.C. Corps orders No. 326. dated 28.7.16. No. 28636 Dr. BARRETT W. A.S.C. awarded 7 days No. 2 Field Punishment.	
"	9.8.16		16 sick evacuated from MERICOURT to No. 7 Vety. Hospital.	
"	10.8.16		Nothing to record.	
"	11.8.16		15 sick evacuated to No. 7 Vety. Hospital.	
"	12.8.16		Nothing to record	
"	13.8.16		"	
"	14.8.16		"	
"	15.8.16		9 sick evacuated from MERICOURT to No. 7 Vety. Hospital.	
"	16.8.16	9 A.M.	Section marched from VILLE-SUR-ANCRE	
GROVETOWN	16.8.16	11 A.M.	arrived GROVETOWN 11 A.M. 5 Miles.	
"	17.8.16		Advanced Dressing Station posted at BILLON FARM.	
"	18.8.16		Nothing to record.	

2449 Wt. W14957/M90 750,000 1/16 J.B.C. & A. Forms/C.2118/12.

Instructions regarding War Diaries and Intelligence Summaries are contained in F. S. Regs., Part II. and the Staff Manual respectively. Title Pages will be prepared in manuscript.

No. 2

WAR DIARY of No. XI Mobile Veterinary Section 3rd Division

or

INTELLIGENCE SUMMARY

(Erase heading not required.)

by C. Sewell Capt. A.V.C.

Army Form C. 2118.

Place	Date	Hour	Summary of Events and Information	Remarks and references to Appendices
GROVETOWN	19.8.16		No. 2279 Pte. WARREN C. joined Section from No. 8 Vety. Hospital, No. 2638	
			Pte LUXON A.J. promoted to rank of Corporal, with effect from 15.7.16. L.C.O. No. 55.	
"	20.8.16		40 sick evacuated from MERICOURT to No. 7 Vety. Hospital. No. 9404 Rfn.	
			WHITTAKER W. attached to Section for Vety. Course from 20th Batt. K.R.R. Corps.	
			Advanced Dressing Station withdrawn from BILLON FARM.	
"	21.8.16	10 A.M.	Section marched to TREUX	
TREUX	21.8.16	12 A.M.	arrived at 12 A.M. 5 Miles.	
"	22.8.16	10.40 A.M.	Section marched from TREUX, + evacuated 16 sick from MERICOURT to No 7 Vety. Hospital,	
FLESSELLES	22.8.16	7.30 P.M.	arrived FLESSELLES 7:30 P.M. marching via, MERICOURT, CORBIE, BUSSEY, COISY BERTANGLES. 20 Miles	
"	23.8.16.	8. A.M.	Section marched from FLESSELLES 8 A.M. arrived	
BERNAVILLE	23.8.16	1.15 P.M.	Via CANAPLES, BENEIVL 10 Miles, No. 3548 Pte JOHNSL admitted to Hospital.	
"	24.8.16		Nothing to record.	
"	25.8.16.	10 A.M.	Section marched from BERNAVILLE arrived	
FROHEN-LE-GRAND	25.8.16	1. P.M.	travelling LE MEILLARD. 6 Miles.	
"	26.8.16.	10 A.M.	marched from FROHEN-LE-GRAND, + arrived FLERS at	
FLERS	26.8.16	2 P.M.	Via. VILLERS L'HOPITAL, VACQUERIE-LE-BOUCQ, BOUBERS-SUR-CANCHE 10 Miles	
"	27.8.16	10 A.M.	Marched to MONCHY-CAYOUX arrived	
MONCHY CAYOUX	27.8.16	2:15 P.M.	Marching via CROISETTE, SIRACOURT, CROIX HERNICOURT, 10 Miles.	

2449 Wt. W14957/M90 750,000 1/16 J.B.C. & A. Forms/C.2118/12.

Instructions regarding War Diaries and Intelligence Summaries are contained in F. S. Regs., Part II. and the Staff Manual respectively. Title Pages will be prepared in manuscript.

WAR DIARY No. 3 of No. XI Mobile Veterinary Section 3rd Division

or

~~INTELLIGENCE SUMMARY~~

(Erase heading not required.)

by Edwell Capt. A.V.C.

Army Form C. 2118.

Place	Date	Hour	Summary of Events and Information	Remarks and references to Appendices
MONCHY-CAYEUX	28.8.16	7 A.M.	Section marched from Billets in MONCHY-CAYEUX + arrived at Billets in	
NOEUX LES MINES	28.8.16	5.15 P.M.	Marching via HESTRUS, VALHUON, LATHIEULOYE, BAJUS, CAMTE, HOUDAIN + RUITZ, Distance 19 Miles.	
"	29.8.16		Nothing to record.	
"	30.8.16		Nothing to record.	
"	31.8.16		5 sick horses evacuated by Barge from BETHUNE to No. 23 Vety. Hospital. Brig. General Moore, accompanied by an American Veterinary Officer, D.D.V.S. 1st Army, + A.D.V.S. 3rd Division inspected the Section 12:15 P.M.	

Instructions regarding War Diaries and Intelligence Summaries are contained in F. S. Regs., Part II. and the Staff Manual respectively. Title Pages will be prepared in manuscript.

WAR DIARY ~~or~~ No. 1 ~~INTELLIGENCE SUMMARY~~

(Erase heading not required.)

No. XI Mobile Veterinary Section 3rd Division
by E. Sewell Capt. A. V. C.

Army Form C. 2118.

Vol 26

Place	Date	Hour	Summary of Events and Information	Remarks and references to Appendices
NOEUX-LES-MINES.	1.9.16		No. 8264 Pte. SMITH P. joined the Section from No 8 Vety. Hospital.	
"	2.9.16		Nothing to record.	
"	3.9.16		5 sick horses entrained at NOEUX-LES-MINES for No. 13 Vety. Hospital.	
"	4.9.16		Nothing to record.	
"	5.9.16		4 sick horses entrained at NOEUX-LES-MINES for No. 13 Vety. Hospital	
"	6.9.16		28 sick horses evacuated by Barge from BETHUNE to No. 23 Vety. Hospital	
"	7.9.16.		Nothing to record.	
"	8.9.16		5 sick horses entrained at NOEUX-LES-MINES for No. 17 Vety. Hospital.	
"	9.9.16	}	Nothing to record.	
"	10.9.16	}		
"	11.9.16	}		
"	12.9.16		9 sick horses evacuated by Barge from BETHUNE to No. 23 Vety. Hospital.	
"	13.9.16		Nothing to record.	
"	14.9.16		61 sick horses entrained at NOEUX-LES-MINES for No. 13 Vety. Hospital.	
"	15.9.16	}	Nothing to record.	
"	16.9.16	}		
"	17.9.16	}		
"	18.9.16		124 sick horses entrained at NOEUX-LES-MINES for No. 13 Vety. Hospital.	
"	19.9.16		33 sick horses evacuated by Barge from BETHUNE for No. 23 Vety. Hospital.	

2449 Wt. W14957/M90 750,000 1/16 J.B.C. & A. Forms/C.2118/12.

Instructions regarding War Diaries and Intelligence Summaries are contained in F. S. Regs., Part II. and the Staff Manual respectively. Title Pages will be prepared in manuscript.

WAR DIARY No. 2 of No. XI Mobile Veterinary Section 37th Division

~~or~~

~~INTELLIGENCE SUMMARY~~

(Erase heading not required.)

by ~~[illegible]~~ E. Sewell. Capt. A.V.C.

Army Form C. 2118.

Place	Date	Hour	Summary of Events and Information	Remarks and references to Appendices
NOEUX-LES-MINES.	19.9.16		No. S.R. 234 Dr. WATSON. M. A.S.C. + No Pte McNAUGHTON R.H. Attached to Section with G.S. Waggon + experimental magnet for clearing roads.	
"	20.9.16		No. 4320 S.S. WADDELL. G. promoted to the rank of paid acting Shoeing Smith Corporal with effect from 2.9.16. ~~D.V.S. [illegible]~~ A.V.C. Corps orders 576. dated 15.9.16	
"	21.9.16		Nothing to record.	
"	22.9.16		Two horses belonging to 40th Division hit by shell fire from own anti aircraft guns destroyed + sold for 300 francs to M. Van Rompaey NOEUX-LES-MINES.	
"	23.9.16		Section marched to NOEUX-LES-MINES Station + entrained 14 sick for No. 13 Vety. Hospital	
"	24.9.16	9.15 AM	Section marched via BRUAY to LA PUGNOYE distance 7 miles	
LA PUGNOYE	24.9.16	12.15 PM	Nothing to record.	
"	25.9.16	10 AM	Section marched via AUCHEL, CAUCHY, FERFAY, ESTREE-LE-BLANCHE, to billets at THEROUANNE distance 18 miles.	
THEROUANNE	25.9.16	5.45 PM	Nothing to record.	
"	26.9.16		Nothing to record.	
"	27.9.16		8 sick evacuated to No. 23 Vety. Hospital ST. OMER by Road.	
"	28.9.16		Nothing to record.	
"	29.9.16			
"	30.9.16		5 sick evacuated by Road to No. 23 Vety. Hospital St. OMER.	

2449 Wt. W14957/M90 750,000 1/16 J.B.C. & A. Forms/C.2118/12.

Army Form C. 2118.

No. 1

WAR DIARY of No. XI Mobile Veterinary Section 3rd Division

or

~~INTELLIGENCE SUMMARY~~

(*Erase heading not required.*)

by C. Sewell Capt. A.V.C.

Vol 27

Instructions regarding War Diaries and Intelligence Summaries are contained in F. S. Regs., Part II. and the Staff Manual respectively. Title Pages will be prepared in manuscript.

Place	Date	Hour	Summary of Events and Information	Remarks and references to Appendices
THEROUANNE	1.10.16		No. 3039 Pte. BEALE W.S. Joined the Section from No. 5 Vety. Hospital. 11 Sick evacuated by road to No. 23 Vety. Hospital St. OMER.	
"	2.10.16		19 Sick evacuated to No. 23 Vety. Hospital St. OMER. No. 9404 Pte. WHITTAKER rejoined his unit on completion of Vety. Course.	
"	3.10.16		Nothing to record.	
"	4.10.16		42 Sick evacuated to No. 23 Vety. Hospital St. OMER.	
"	5.10.16	7 A.M.	Section marched from THEROUANNE, via ESTEES-BLANCHE, CUHEM, FONTAINE	
TENEUR	5.10.16	3 P.M.	HEUCHIN, BERGUENEUSE TENEUR arriving 3 P.M.	
"	6.10.16	6 A.M.	Section marched from TENEUR, at 6 A.M. via St. POL, HERLIN-LE-SEC, BUNEVILLE	
BERLENCOURT	6.10.16	3 P.M.	ESTREES-WAMIN arrived BERLENCOURT 3 P.M.	
"	7.10.16	7 A.M.	Section marched via BEAUDRICOURT, MONDICOURT, PAS, AUTHIE,	
BERTRANCOURT	7.10.16	6:30 P.M.	LOUVENCOURT arriving BERTRANCOURT 6:30 P.M.	
"	8.10.16		Nothing to record.	
"	9.10.16	9:45 A.M.	Section marched to Billet at ACHEUX arriving 11 A.M.	
ACHEUX	10.10.16		No. 281 Pte. NOCKE, proceeded to No. 38 Infantry Base depot ETAPLES authority D.A.G. C.R. No. 27294A. 24 Sick evacuated from ACHEUX to No. 7 Vety. Hospital.	
~~"~~	~~11.10.1~~			
"	11.10.16		12 Sick evacuated to No. 7 Vety. Hospital.	
"	12.10.16		Nothing to record.	
"	13.10.16			
"	14.10.16		19 Sick evacuated from ACHEUX to No. 7 Vety. Hospital.	
"	15.10.16		Nothing to record.	

2449 Wt. W14957/M90 750,000 1/16 J.B.C. & A. Forms/C.2118/12.

Army Form C. 2118.

Instructions regarding War Diaries and Intelligence Summaries are contained in F. S. Regs., Part II. and the Staff Manual respectively. Title Pages will be prepared in manuscript.

No. 2

WAR DIARY of No. XI Mobile Veterinary Section 3rd Division

~~or~~

~~INTELLIGENCE SUMMARY~~

(Erase heading not required.)

by E Atwell Capt. A.V.C.

Place	Date	Hour	Summary of Events and Information	Remarks and references to Appendices
ACHEUX.	16.10.16		Advanced Dressing Station posted at COLINCAMPS.	
"	17.10.16		Nothing to record.	
"	18.10.16		21 sick sent to No. 7 Vety. Hospital. at 2:30 P.M. Section marched to Billets at BUS. arriving 4.P.M.	
BUS	19.10.16		Nothing to record.	
"	20.10.16		40 sick evacuated to No. 7 Vety. Hospital.	
"	21.10.16		Nothing to record	
"	22.10.16		25 sick evacuated to No. 7 Vety. Hospital.	
"	23.10.16		Nothing to record. (23.10.16–24.10.16)	
"	24.10.16			
"	25.10.16		16 sick evacuated to No. 7 Vety. Hospital	
"	26.10.16		Nothing to record.	
"	27.10.16		15 sick + 1 Cast, evacuated to No. 7 Vety. Hospital.	
"	28.10.16		Nothing to record.	
"	29.10.16		23 sick evacuated to No. 7 Vety. Hospital.	
"	30.10.16		Advanced Dressing Station withdrawn from COLINCAMPS.	
"	31.10.16		14 sick evacuated to No. 7 Vety. Hospital.	

Instructions regarding War Diaries and Intelligence Summaries are contained in F. S. Regs., Part II. and the Staff Manual respectively. Title Pages will be prepared in manuscript.

WAR DIARY No 1
~~or~~
INTELLIGENCE SUMMARY
of No. XI Mobile Veterinary Section 3rd Division by C. [illegible] Capt. A.V.C.

(Erase heading not required.)

Army Form C. 2118.

Vol 28

Place	Date	Hour	Summary of Events and Information	Remarks and references to Appendices
BUS-LES-ARTOIS	1.11.16		Nothing to record.	
"	2.11.16		Nothing to record.	
"	3.11.16		32 sick evacuated to No. 7 Vety. Hospital from BELLE-EGLISE Station	
"	4.11.16		Nothing to record	
"	5.11.16		22 sick evacuated to No. 7 Vety. Hospital, "	
"	6.11.16		Nothing to record.	
"	7.11.16		48 sick evacuated to No. 7 Vety. Hospital, "	
"	8.11.16		Nothing to record.	
"	9.11.16		16 sick evacuated to No. 7 Vety. Hospital, "	
"	10.11.16		26 sick evacuated to No. 7 Vety. Hospital "	
"	11.11.16		Nothing to record.	
"	12.11.16		28 sick evacuated to No. 7 Vety. Hospital. Advanced Dressing Station posted at COLINCAMPS.	
"	13.11.16		Nothing to record	
"	14.11.16		25 sick evacuated to No. 7 Vety. Hospital. from BELLE-EGLISE Station	
"	15.11.16		Advanced Dressing Station withdrawn from COLINCAMPS.	
"	16.11.16		33 sick evacuated to No. 7 Vety. Hospital	
"	17.11.16		34 sick evacuated to No. 7 Vety. Hospital No. S.E. 10577 Cpl. STOKES. W. H. [illegible] to 16 Batt. Rifle Brigade, 4/7 Inf. Base depot HAVRE. Auth. D.A.G. C.R. No. 4101[illegible]A.	
"	18.11.16		Nothing to record	
"	19.11.16		32 sick evacuated to No. 7 Vety. Hospital, from BELLE-EGLISE Station.	
"	20.11.16		Nothing to record.	

Instructions regarding War Diaries and Intelligence Summaries are contained in F. S. Regs., Part II. and the Staff Manual respectively. Title Pages will be prepared in manuscript.

Army Form C. 2118.

WAR DIARY No. 2
or
~~INTELLIGENCE SUMMARY~~ of No. XI Mobile Veterinary Section 3rd Division by Elwell Capt. A.V.C.

(*Erase heading not required.*)

Place	Date	Hour	Summary of Events and Information	Remarks and references to Appendices
BUS-LES-ARTOIS	21.11.16		29 sick evacuated to No. 7 Vety. Hospital.	
"	22.11.16		Nothing to record.	
"	23.11.16		40 sick evacuated to No. 7 Vety. Hospital.	
"	24.11.16		32 sick " " "	
"	25.11.16		No. SE.8244 Pte. SMITH. P. proceeded on leave to England.	
"	26.11.16		26 sick evacuated to No. 7 Vety. Hospital.	
"	27.11.16		No. 74603 Dr. LEAVER. W. evacuated to Base Hospital	
"	28.11.16		13 sick evacuated to No. 7 Vety. Hospital.	
"	29.11.16			
"	30.11.16		16 sick evacuated to No. 7 Vety. Hospital. S.E. No. 1517 Pte. BOYALL O. joined the section from No. 2 Vety. Hospital.	

2449 Wt. W14957/M90 750,000 1/16 J.B.C. & A. Forms/C.2118/12.

Instructions regarding War Diaries and Intelligence Summaries are contained in F. S. Regs., Part II. and the Staff Manual respectively. Title Pages will be prepared in manuscript.

Army Form C. 2118.

No. 1 WAR DIARY ~~or INTELLIGENCE SUMMARY~~

of No. XI Mobile Veterinary Section 3rd Division by E Lowell. Capt. A.V.C. Vol 29

(Erase heading not required.)

Place	Date	Hour	Summary of Events and Information	Remarks and references to Appendices
BUS-LES-ARTOIS.	1.12.16		Nothing to record.	
"	2.12.16		Nothing to record.	
"	3.12.16		Nothing to record.	
"	4.12.16		32 sick evacuated to No. 7 Vety. Hospital from BEAUSSART.	
"	5.12.16		Nothing to record.	
"	6.12.16		Nothing to record.	
"	7.12.16		Nothing to record.	
"	8.12.16		Nothing to record.	
"	9.12.16		22 sick evacuated to No. 22 Vety. Hospital.	
"	10.12.16		Nothing to record.	
"	11.12.16		No. 28636 Dr. BARRETT W. admitted to hospital. 7 sick evacuated to No. 22 Vety. Hospital.	
"	12.12.16		Nothing to record.	
"	13.12.16		21 sick evacuated to No. 22 Vety. Hospital. A.S.C. attd. Dr. BARRETT W. evacuated & struck off strength.	
"	14.12.16		Nothing to record.	
"	15.12.16		Nothing to record.	
"	16.12.16		57 sick evacuated to No. 22 Vety. Hospital	
"	17.12.16		Nothing to record.	
"	18.12.16		Nothing to record.	
"	19.12.16		2 sick evacuated to No. 22 Vety. Hospital	
"	20.12.16		64 sick evacuated to No. 22 Vety. Hospital	

2449 Wt. W14957/M90 750,000 1/16 J.B.C. & A. Forms/C.2118/12.

Army Form C. 2118.

Instructions regarding War Diaries and Intelligence Summaries are contained in F. S. Regs., Part II. and the Staff Manual respectively. Title Pages will be prepared in manuscript.

No. 2

WAR DIARY
or
~~INTELLIGENCE~~ SUMMARY
of No. XI Mobile Veterinary Section 3rd Division
(*Erase heading not required.*)

by [illegible] Sewell Capt. A.V.C.

Place	Date	Hour	Summary of Events and Information	Remarks and references to Appendices
BUS-LES-ARTOIS	21.12.16		Nothing to record.	
"	22.12.16		Nothing to record.	
"	23.12.16		4 Sick evacuated to No. 22 Vety. Hospital	
"	24.12.16		Nothing to record	
"	25.12.16		Nothing to record	
"	26.12.16		8264 Pte. SMITH P. admitted to Hospital.	
"	27.12.16		61 Sick evacuated to No. 22 Vety. Hospital	
"	28.12.16		Nothing to record.	
"	29.12.16		Nothing to record.	
"	30.12.16		No. 8264 Pte. SMITH P. evacuated & struck off strength	
"	31.12.16		57 Sick evacuated to No. 22 Vety. Hospital.	

2449 Wt. W14957/M90 750,000 1/16 J.B.C. & A. Forms/C.2118/12.

3RD DIVISION

NO.11 MOBILE VETERINARY SECTION

JAN - DEC 1917

No. 1

Army Form C. 2118.

Instructions regarding War Diaries and Intelligence Summaries are contained in F. S. Regs., Part II. and the Staff Manual respectively. Title pages will be prepared in manuscript.

WAR DIARY

~~or~~ of No. 11 Mobile Veterinary Section 3rd Division

~~INTELLIGENCE SUMMARY.~~

(Erase heading not required.)

by [illegible]

Vol 30

Place	Date	Hour	Summary of Events and Information	Remarks and references to Appendices
RUS-LES-ARTOIS	1.1.17		Nothing to record	
	2.1.17		No: 13483 Pte. CURSON G. admitted to hospital	
"	3.1.17		No. 3483 Pte CURSON G. evacuated to C.C.S.	
"	4.1.17		39 sick evacuated to 22 Vety. Hospital.	
"	5.1.17		Nothing to record.	
"	6.1.17		8 sick evacuated to No. 22 Vety. Hospital.	
"	7.1.17		Nothing to record.	
RUS-LES-ARTOIS	8.1.17	7.45 AM	Section moved & arrived at	
ST OUEN	8.1.17	4.30 PM		
"	9.1.17		Nothing to record	
"	10.1.17		Nothing to record.	
"	11.1.17		Nothing to record.	
"	12.1.17		8 sick evacuated to No. 22 Vety. Hospital. No. 7128 Pte. HYDE. A from 18 Division M.V.S. No. S3/024358 Dr. MORRISH A.S.C. " T2/14958 Dr. LATHAM C. A. A.S.C. from [illegible]	Rejoined [illegible] M.V.S.
"	13.1.17		Nothing to record.	
	14.1.17		Nothing to record.	
"	15.1.17		14 sick evacuated to 22 Vety. Hospital.	
	16.1.17		Nothing to record.	
	17.1.17		40 sick evacuated to No. 22 Vety. Hospital.	
	18.1.17		Nothing to record.	
	19.1.17		11 sick evacuated to No. 22 Vety. Hospital	

A5834 Wt. W4973/M687 750,000 8/16 D. D. & L. Ltd. Forms/C.2118/13.

Instructions regarding War Diaries and Intelligence Summaries are contained in F. S. Regs., Part II. and the Staff Manual respectively. Title Pages will be prepared in manuscript.

No. 2

WAR DIARY ~~or~~ of No. XI Mobile Vety. Section 3rd. Division

~~INTELLIGENCE SUMMARY~~

(Erase heading not required.)

G. Chewell. Capt. A.V.C

Army Form C. 2118.

Place	Date	Hour	Summary of Events and Information	Remarks and references to Appendices
ST. OUEN.	20.1.17		12 sick evacuated to No. 22 Vety. Hospital.	
"	21.1.17		Nothing to record.	
"	22.1.17		Nothing to record.	
"	23.1.17		36 sick evacuated to No. 22 Vety. Hospital. No. 2635 Sgt. LUXON. A.T. proceeded to join No. 27 M.V.S. on promotion from Rank of Corporal.	
"	24.1.17		13 sick evacuated to No. 22 Vety. Hospital	
"	25.1.17		No. 2300 Pte. PARTRIDGE. G. reported for duty from No. 5 Vety. Hospital	
"	26.1.17		12 sick evacuated to No 22 Vety Hospital.	
"	27.1.17		Nothing to record.	
"	28.1.17		Nothing to record.	
"	29.1.17	8 A.M.	Section moved to	
SARTON	29.1.17	2:30 P.M.	arrived	
"	30.1.17	9 A.M.	Section moved to CONCHY-SUR-CANCHE arrived 4.30 P.M.	
CONCHY-SUR-CANCHE	"	4.30 P.M.	Nothing to record.	

2449 Wt. W14957/M90 750,000 1/16 J.B.C. & A. Forms/C.2118/12.

Instructions regarding War Diaries and Intelligence Summaries are contained in F. S. Regs., Part II. and the Staff Manual respectively. Title Pages will be prepared in manuscript.

No. 1
WAR DIARY
or
~~INTELLIGENCE SUMMARY~~
of No XI Mobile Veterinary Section
3rd Division
by [illegible] Capt. A.V.C.

(Erase heading not required.)

Army Form C. 2118.

Vol 31

Place	Date	Hour	Summary of Events and Information	Remarks and references to Appendices
CONCHY-SUR-CANCHE	1.2.17	9.30AM	Section moved and arrived at	
LA COMTE	1.2.17	6.P.M.		
"	2.2.17		Nothing to record.	
"	3.2.17		Nothing to record	
"	4.2.17		Nothing to record.	
"	5.2.17		Nothing to record.	
"	6.2.17		Nothing to record.	
"	7.2.17		Nothing to record.	
"	8.2.17	6.A.M	Section moved and arrived a	
CANETTEMONT	8.2.17	11.A.M		
"	9.2.17		Nothing to record	
"	10.2.17		Nothing to record	
"	11.2.17		Nothing to record	
"	12.2.17		Nothing to record	
"	13.2.17		Nothing to record	
"	14.2.17		Nothing to record	
"	15.2.17		55 Sick evacuated to No 22 Veterinary Hospital from FREVENT.	
"	16.2.17		Nothing to record	
"	17.2.17		Nothing to record	
"	18.2.17		Nothing to record	
"	19.2.17		Nothing to record	
"	20.2.17		Nothing to record.	

2449 Wt. W14957/M90 750,000 1/16 J.B.C. & A. Forms/C.2118/12.

Instructions regarding War Diaries and Intelligence Summaries are contained in F. S. Regs., Part II. and the Staff Manual respectively. Title Pages will be prepared in manuscript.

Army Form C. 2118.

No. 2.

WAR DIARY
or
~~INTELLIGENCE~~ SUMMARY
of No XI Mobile Veterinary Section 3rd Division

(Erase heading not required.)

by [illegible] Capt. AVC

Place	Date	Hour	Summary of Events and Information	Remarks and references to Appendices
CANETTEMONT	21.2.17		Nothing to record.	
"	22.2.17		23 Sick evacuated to No 22 Veterinary Hospital	
"	23.2.17	9.30 A.M.	Section moved and arrived at	
AVESNES-LE COMTE	23.2.17	12.15 P.M.		
"	24.2.17		Nothing to record	
"	25.		Nothing to record.	
"	26		Nothing to record.	
"	27		Nothing to record	
"	28		Nothing to record.	

2449 Wt. W14957/M90 750,000 1/16 J.B.C. & A. Forms/C.2118/12.

Instructions regarding War Diaries and Intelligence Summaries are contained in F. S. Regs., Part II. and the Staff Manual respectively. Title Pages will be prepared in manuscript.

No. 1

WAR DIARY

or

~~INTELLIGENCE~~ SUMMARY

of No XI Mobile Veterinary Section

(Erase heading not required.)

by [signature] Capt. A.V.C.

Vol 32

Army Form C. 2118.

Place	Date	Hour	Summary of Events and Information	Remarks and references to Appendices
AVESNES-LE-COMTE	1.3.17		45 Sick evacuated to 22 Veterinary Hospital from SAULTY.	
"	2.3.17		Nothing to record.	
"	3.3.17		Nothing to record.	
"	4.3.17		Nothing to record.	
"	5.3.17		Nothing to record.	
"	6.3.17		Nothing to record.	
"	7.3.17		Nothing to record.	
"	8.3.17		33 Sick evacuated to 22 Veterinary Hospital from SAULTY. S.E Pte MATHEWS. C.J., A.V.C. reported for duty at No XI Mobile Vety Section from No 9 Veterinary Hospital.	
"	9.3.17		Nothing to record	
"	10.3.17		Nothing to record	
"	11.3.17		Nothing to record	
"	12.3.17		Nothing to record.	
"	13.3.17		Nothing to record.	
"	14.3.17		8 Sick evacuated to 22 Veterinary Hospital from TINQUES.	
"	15.3.17		Nothing to record.	
"	16.3.17		Nothing to record.	

No. 2.

Instructions regarding War Diaries and Intelligence Summaries are contained in F. S. Regs., Part II. and the Staff Manual respectively. Title pages will be prepared in manuscript.

WAR DIARY ~~or~~ of XI Mobile Veterinary Section
~~INTELLIGENCE SUMMARY.~~

(Erase heading not required.)

Army Form C. 2118.

by [signature] Capt. A.V.C.

Place	Date	Hour	Summary of Events and Information	Remarks and references to Appendices
AVESNES-LE-COMTE	17.3.17		26 Sick evacuated to 22 Veterinary Hospital from SAULTY.	
"	18.3.17		Nothing to record.	
"	19.3.17		S.E. 3518 PTE. SQUIRES J. admitted to Hospital.	
"	20.3.17		S.E. 3518 PTE SQUIRES J evacuated to Casualty Clearing Station.	
"	21.3.17		28 Sick evacuated to 22 Veterinary Hospital from TINQUES	
"	22.3.17		Nothing to record.	
"	23.3.17		Nothing to record.	
"	24.3.17		16 Sick evacuated to 22 Veterinary Hospital from SAULTY	
"	25.3.17		Nothing to record	
"	26.3.17		Nothing to record.	
"	27.3.17		Nothing to record.	
"	28.3.17		20 Sick evacuated to 22 Veterinary Hospital from TINQUES	
"	29.3.17		Nothing to record	
"	30.3.17		Nothing to record.	
"	31.3.17		10 Sick evacuated to 22 Veterinary Hospital from SAULTY.	

A5834 Wt. W4973/M687 750,000 8/16 D. D. & L. Ltd. Forms/C.2118/13.

No. 1.

Vol 33

Army Form C. 2118.

Instructions regarding War Diaries and Intelligence Summaries are contained in F. S. Regs., Part II. and the Staff Manual respectively. Title pages will be prepared in manuscript.

WAR DIARY
or
~~INTELLIGENCE~~ SUMMARY.
(Erase heading not required.)

OF XI Mobile Veterinary Section

[illegible] Capt. A.V.C.

Place	Date	Hour	Summary of Events and Information	Remarks and references to Appendices
AVESNES-LE-COMTE	1.4.17		418 Sergt. Jordan A. is taken on strength of Section from No. 5 Veterinary Hospital	
		10.a.m	Section moved and arrived at	
WANQUETIN	1.4.17	11.15 a.m.		
"	2.4.17		5295. Staff Sergt. Munson W. L. proceeded to No. 6 Veterinary Hospital	
"	3.4.17		Advanced Dressing Station posted at ARRAS.	
"	4.4.17		8 Sick evacuated to 22 Veterinary Hospital from SAULTY	
"	5.4.17		Nothing to record.	
"	6.4.17		Nothing to record.	
"	7.4.17		112 Sick evacuated to 22 Veterinary Hospital from GOUY.	
"	8.4.17		Nothing to record.	
"	9.4.17		24 Sick evacuated to 22 Veterinary Hospital from GOUY.	
"	10.4.17		Nothing to record.	
"	11.4.17		31 Sick evacuated to 22 Veterinary Hospital from AGNEZ.	
"	11.4.17	3.p.m	Section moved and arrived at	
ARRAS	11.4.17	5.p.m		
"	12.4.17		Nothing to record.	
"	13.4.17		31 Sick evacuated to 22 Veterinary Hospital from AGNEZ.	

A5834 Wt. W4973/M687 750,000 8/16 D. D. & L. Ltd. Forms/C.2118/13.

No 2

Instructions regarding War Diaries and Intelligence Summaries are contained in F. S. Regs., Part II. and the Staff Manual respectively. Title pages will be prepared in manuscript.

WAR DIARY
~~or~~
~~INTELLIGENCE~~ SUMMARY.
(Erase heading not required.)

OF XI Mobile Veterinary Section

by [illegible] Capt. A.V.C.

Army Form C. 2118.

Place	Date	Hour	Summary of Events and Information	Remarks and references to Appendices
ARRAS	14.4.17		31 Sick evacuated to 22 Veterinary Hospital from AGNEZ	
"	15.4.17		13 Sick evacuated to 22 Veterinary Hospital from AGNEZ	
"	16.4.17	3.P.M.	Section moved from ARRAS and arrived at	
DAINVILLE	16.4.17	4.P.M.		
"	17.4.17		19 Sick evacuated to 22 Veterinary Hospital from AGNEZ.	
"	18.4.17		478 SERGT JORDAN. A, 834 PTE BENNET W and 1349 PTE ROOKS T. proceeded to join VI Corps Mobile Veterinary Detachment.	
			17154 PTE WADE J reported for duty from No 6 Veterinary Hospital	
"	19.4.17		Nothing to record.	
"	20.4.17		24 Sick evacuated to 22 Veterinary Hospital from AGNEZ.	
"	21.4.17		Nothing to record	
"	22.4.17		20 Sick evacuated from AGNEZ to 22 Veterinary Hospital	
"	23.4.17		Nothing to record.	
"	24.4.17		13 Sick evacuated to 22 Veterinary Hospital from ARRAS.	
"	25.4.17		Nothing to record.	
"	26.4.17		20 Sick evacuated to 22 Veterinary Hospital from ARRAS. 6269 Sergt GREEN G reported for duty from 24 Mobile Veterinary Section	

A5834 Wt. W4973/M687 750,000 8/16 D. D. & L. Ltd. Forms/C.2118/13.

Instructions regarding War Diaries and Intelligence Summaries are contained in F. S. Regs., Part II. and the Staff Manual respectively. Title pages will be prepared in manuscript.

Army Form C. 2118.

No 3

WAR DIARY
or
~~INTELLIGENCE SUMMARY.~~
(Erase heading not required.)

OF XI Mobile Veterinary Section

Place	Date	Hour	Summary of Events and Information	Remarks and references to Appendices
DAINVILLE	27.4.17	10. a.m.	Section moved from DAINVILLE and arrived at	
ARRAS	27.4.17	11.30.a.m.		
			1173 Staff Sergt BRADSHAW R proceeded to No 9 Veterinary Hospital	
			5447 Pte SPRINGTHORP R reported for duty from No 10 Veterinary Hospital	
"	28.4.17		32 Sick evacuated from ARRAS to 22 Veterinary Hospital	
			2 N.C.O's and 12 men of Base Conducting Party reported for duty from 18th Mobile Veterinary Section	
"	29.4.17		2 men of Base Conducting Party reported for duty from 18th Mobile Veterinary Section	
"	30.4.17		12 Sick evacuated from ARRAS to 22 Veterinary Hospital	
			1 N.C.O and 5 men of Base Conducting Party reported for duty from 18th Mobile Veterinary Section	

A5834 Wt. W4973/M687 750,000 8/16 D. D. & L. Ltd. Forms/C.2118/13.

Instructions regarding War Diaries and Intelligence Summaries are contained in F. S. Regs., Part II. and the Staff Manual respectively. Title pages will be prepared in manuscript.

No 1

WAR DIARY ~~or~~ OF XI Mobile Veterinary Section

~~INTELLIGENCE SUMMARY.~~ by [signature] Capt A.V.C.

(Erase heading not required.)

Army Form C. 2118.

Vol 34

Place	Date	Hour	Summary of Events and Information	Remarks and references to Appendices
ARRAS	1.5.17		28 sick evacuated to 22 Veterinary Hospital from ARRAS.	
"	2.5.17		7 sick evacuated to 22 Veterinary Hospital from ARRAS.	
			No 2300 Pte PARTRIDGE G admitted to Hospital	
"	3.5.17		22 sick evacuated from ARRAS to 22 Veterinary Hospital	
"	4.5.17		Advanced Dressing Station posted	
"	5.5.17		8 sick evacuated to 22 Veterinary Hospital from ARRAS.	
"	6.5.17		Nothing to record	
"	7.5.17		Nothing to record.	
"	8.5.17		40 sick evacuated to 22 Veterinary Hospital from AGNEZ.	
"	9.5.17		Nothing to record.	
"	10.5.17		Nothing to record.	
"	11.5.17		8 sick evacuated from ARRAS to 22 Veterinary Hospital	
"	12.5.17		Section moved to G32a 8.7.	
"	13.5.17		13 sick evacuated from ARRAS to 22 Veterinary Hospital. Advanced Dressing Station withdrawn.	
"	14.5.17		Nothing to record.	

Army Form C. 2118.

No. 2

WAR DIARY ~~or~~ OF XI Mobile Veterinary Section

~~INTELLIGENCE SUMMARY.~~ by [signature] Capt A.V.C.

(Erase heading not required.)

Instructions regarding War Diaries and Intelligence Summaries are contained in F. S. Regs., Part II. and the Staff Manual respectively. Title pages will be prepared in manuscript.

Place	Date	Hour	Summary of Events and Information	Remarks and references to Appendices
ARRAS	15.5.17	9.45AM.	Section moved from ARRAS to AGNEZ	
AGNEZ	15.5.17	11.a.m	Section arrived at AGNEZ	
"	16.5.17		Nothing to record	
"	17.5.17		Nothing to record.	
"	18.5.17		10 sick evacuated from AGNEZ to 22 Veterinary Hospital. No 2300 Pte PARTRIDGE G struck off the strength of section. 834 Pte BENNETT. W & 1349 Pte ROOKS T reported from VI Corps M.V.S.	
"	19.5.17.		Base Conducting Party of 3 N.C.O's and 19 men handed over to 23rd Mobile Vety Section	
"	19.5.17	10.a.m	Section moved to LIGNEREUIL	
LIGNEREUIL	19.5.17	1.P.M.	Section arrived at LIGNEREUIL	
"	20.5.17		Nothing to record.	
"	21.5.17		No 17154 Pte WADE J admitted to Hospital	
"	22.5.17		Nothing to record	
"	23.5.17		Nothing to record	
"	24.5.17		Nothing to record	
"	25.5.17		Nothing to record.	
"	26.5.17		6 sick evacuated to 22 Veterinary Hospital from FREVENT.	

2353 Wt. W2544/1454 700,000 5/15 D. D. & L. A.D.S.S./Forms/C. 2118.

Instructions regarding War Diaries and Intelligence Summaries are contained in F. S. Regs., Part II. and the Staff Manual respectively. Title pages will be prepared in manuscript.

No 3.

WAR DIARY ~~or~~ OF XI Mobile Veterinary Section

~~**INTELLIGENCE SUMMARY**~~. by [signature] Capt A.V.C.

(*Erase heading not required.*)

Army Form C. 2118.

Place	Date	Hour	Summary of Events and Information	Remarks and references to Appendices
LIGNEREUIL	27.5.17		Nothing to record.	
"	28.5.17		478 SERGT. JORDAN A reported for duty from VI Corps Mobile Veterinary Detachment.	
"	29.5.17		Nothing to record.	
"	30.5.17		6 Sick evacuated from FREVENT to 22 Veterinary Hospital.	
			S.E. 6381 Pte RENFREE C reported for duty from No 1 Veterinary Hospital	
"	30.5.17		17154 Pte WADE J rejoined Section from Hospital	
"	31.5.17		Nothing to record.	

Instructions regarding War Diaries and Intelligence Summaries are contained in F. S. Regs., Part II. and the Staff Manual respectively. Title pages will be prepared in manuscript.

No 1

WAR DIARY

~~or~~ of XI Mobile Veterinary Section

~~INTELLIGENCE SUMMARY.~~ by [signature] Capt. AVC

(Erase heading not required.)

Army Form C. 2118.

Place	Date	Hour	Summary of Events and Information	Remarks and references to Appendices
LIGNEREUIL	1.6.17		4 sick evacuated from TINQUES to 22 Veterinary Hospital.	
			No 5868 Pte EDMUNDS H admitted to Hospital	
"	2.6.17	9.30am	Section moved from LIGNEREUIL to	
ACHICOURT	2.6.17	2.30.	ACHICOURT.	
"	3.6.17		Nothing to record.	
"	4.6.17		11 sick evacuated from ARRAS to 22 Veterinary Hospital.	
"	5.6.17		Nothing to record.	
"	6.6.17		23 sick evacuated from ARRAS to 22 Veterinary Hospital. N.C.O and three men proceed to VI Corps Horse Rest Camp.	
"	7.6.17		23 Sick evacuated from ARRAS to 22 Veterinary Hospital	
	8.6.17		Nothing to record.	
	9.6.17		31 Sick evacuated from ARRAS to 22 Veterinary Hospital	
	10.6.17		Nothing to record.	
	11.6.17		16 Sick evacuated from ARRAS to 22 Veterinary Hospital	
	12.6.17		Nothing to record.	
	13.6.17		19 sick evacuated from ARRAS to 22 Veterinary Hospital.	

2353 Wt. W2544/1454 700,000 5/15 D. D. & L. A.D.S.S./Forms/C. 2118.

No 2.

Instructions regarding War Diaries and Intelligence Summaries are contained in F. S. Regs., Part II. and the Staff Manual respectively. Title pages will be prepared in manuscript.

WAR DIARY

or ~~INTELLIGENCE SUMMARY.~~ of XI Mobile Veterinary Section by J. Sewell Capt. A.V.C

(Erase heading not required.)

Army Form C. 2118.

Place	Date	Hour	Summary of Events and Information	Remarks and references to Appendices
ACHICOURT.	14.6.17		Nothing to record.	
"	15.6.17		Nothing to record.	
"	16.6.17		30 sick evacuated from ARRAS to 22 Veterinary Hospital. N.C.O and three men rejoin Section from VI Corps Horse Rest Camp.	
"	17.6.17		Nothing to record.	
"	18.6.17		7 Sick evacuated from ARRAS to 22 Veterinary Hospital	
"	19.6.17		Nothing to record.	
"	20.6.17	9. am	Section moved to LE CAUROY.	
LE CAUROY	20.6.17	3. p.m.		
"	21.6.17		Nothing to record.	
"	22.6.17		No 689 Corpl PETTIT J attached to 76th Infantry Brigade	
"	23.6.17.		3213 Sergt SMALLRIDGE W. reports for duty from 6 Veterinary Hospital. 5868 Pte EDMUNDS. H struck off the strength of Section on being evacuated sick from Divisional area.	
"	24.6.17		478 Sergt Jordan A proceeds to No 6 Veterinary Hospital.	
"	25.6.17		Nothing to record.	
"	26.6.17		Nothing to record.	
"	27.6.17		Nothing to record.	
"	28.6.17		Nothing to record.	
"	29.6.17		Nothing to record.	
"	30.6.17		4 Sick evacuated from FREVENT to 22 Veterinary Hospital. Section moved to HALLOY.-	

1/1/40

Confidential

H.Q. (A) III Divn.

Herewith please find the War Diary re XI Mob Vety Sectn for month of July 1917.

H Campbell Major

DADVS III Divn

D.H.Q.
1/8/17

Instructions regarding War Diaries and Intelligence Summaries are contained in F. S. Regs., Part II. and the Staff Manual respectively. Title pages will be prepared in manuscript.

No. I.

WAR DIARY of XI Mobile Veterinary Section

~~or~~

~~INTELLIGENCE SUMMARY.~~ by [signature] Capt A.V.C

(Erase heading not required.)

Army Form C. 2118.

Vol 36

Place	Date	Hour	Summary of Events and Information	Remarks and references to Appendices
HALLOY	1.7.17	4.30 A.M.	Section moved from HALLOY.	
BIHUCOURT	1.7.17	2.30 P.M.	Section arrived at BIHUCOURT.	
"	2.7.17	-	Nothing to record.	
"	3.7.17		Nothing to record.	
"	4.7.17	10.a.m	Section moved from BIHUCOURT.	
BAPAUME	4.7.17	11.45.a.m	Section arrived at BAPAUME	
"	5.7.17		Nothing to record.	
"	6.7.17		Nothing to record	
"	7.7.17		Nothing to record.	
"	8.7.17		No 687 Corpl Pettit J, A.V.C, struck off the strength of Section on being posted as A.V.C Sergeant to 76th Infantry Brigade	
"	9.7.17		Nothing to record	
"	10.7.17		25 Sick were evacuated from BAPAUME to No 7 Veterinary Hospital	
"	11.7.17		Nothing to record.	
"	12.7.17		Nothing to record.	
"	13.7.17		20 Sick were evacuated from BAPAUME to No 7 Veterinary Hospital.	

2353 Wt. W2544/1454 700,000 5/15 D. D. & L. A.D.S.S./Forms/C. 2118.

Instructions regarding War Diaries and Intelligence Summaries are contained in F. S. Regs., Part II. and the Staff Manual respectively. Title pages will be prepared in manuscript.

No II
WAR DIARY
or
~~INTELLIGENCE SUMMARY~~. of XI Mobile Veterinary Section by [signature] Capt A.V.C

(Erase heading not required.)

Army Form C. 2118.

Place	Date	Hour	Summary of Events and Information	Remarks and references to Appendices
BAPAUME	14.7.17		Nothing to record.	
"	15.7.17		No 19259 Pte BUSHELL J. A.V.C. reported for duty from No 4 Veterinary Hospital	
"	16.7.17		Nothing to record.	
"	17.7.17		15 Sick were evacuated ~~to~~ from BAPAUME to No 7 Veterinary Hospital	
"	18.7.17		Nothing to record	
"	19.7.17		Nothing to record	
"	20.7.17		11 Sick were evacuated to No 7 Veterinary Hospital from BAPAUME	
"	21.7.17		Nothing to record	
"	22.7.17		Nothing to record	
"	23.7.17		Nothing to record.	
"	24.7.17		12 Sick were evacuated from BAPAUME to No 7 Veterinary Hospital. No 520 Staff Sergeant GOODWIN W. A.V.C. and No 7657 Pte RUMMERY H, A.V.C. reported for duty from No 1 Veterinary Hospital	
"	25.7.17		Nothing to record	
"	26.7.17		Nothing to record.	
"	27.7.17		18 Sick were evacuated from BAPAUME to No 7 Veterinary Hospital	

2353 Wt. W2544/1454 700,000 5/15 D. D. & L. A.D.S.S./Forms/C. 2118.

Army Form C. 2118.

Instructions regarding War Diaries and Intelligence Summaries are contained in F. S. Regs., Part II. and the Staff Manual respectively. Title pages will be prepared in manuscript.

No 111

WAR DIARY

or

~~INTELLIGENCE~~ SUMMARY. of XI Mobile Veterinary Section by [illegible] Capt A.V.C

(Erase heading not required.)

Place	Date	Hour	Summary of Events and Information	Remarks and references to Appendices
BAPAUME	28.7.17		Nothing to record.	
"	29.7.17		Nothing to record.	
"	30.7.17		Nothing to record.	
"	31.7.17		22 Sick were evacuated from BAPAUME to No 7 Veterinary Hospital	

2353 Wt. W2544/1454 700,000 5/15 D. D. & L. A.D.S.S./Forms/C. 2118.

Instructions regarding War Diaries and Intelligence Summaries are contained in F. S. Regs., Part II. and the Staff Manual respectively. Title pages will be prepared in manuscript.

WAR DIARY or ~~INTELLIGENCE~~ SUMMARY.

(Erase heading not required.)

of XI Mobile Veterinary Section by [signature] Capt A.V.C.

Army Form C. 2118.

VR 37

Place	Date	Hour	Summary of Events and Information	Remarks and references to Appendices
BAPAUME	1.8.17		Building of Fumigating Chamber for new treatment of Mange is started. Timber and corrugated iron are drawn for the building of stables. Two cases of suspected mange are admitted	
"	2.8.17		Bad weather hampers the work of building stables. Timber and corrugated iron are drawn. Duckboards are collected and laid on paths most frequently used.	
"		6.p.m	N.C.O's and Men are paid	
"	3.8.17		D.A.D.V.S. called and inspected the Section in general and Mange cases in particulars. Made various suggestions for improving the appearance of the Camp as well as economising in space occupied by Section. The alterations suggested were taken in hand immediately. Ten gals of Calc. Sulp. were issued to 23 Batty. Corps Commander's charger was returned cured. One case of susp. Mange was admitted, Bad weather still continues	
"	4.8.17		Heavy rain in the morning. Further progress is made in stable building. D.A.D.V.S. notifies section of arrangements being made to supply two Nissen Huts. Consent of C.R.E. obtained for retaining services of two R.E. men engaged in building SO_2 Chamber. "Turner-Bibby" Horse shoe pad which was put on trial four weeks ago taken off. Reported	

2353 Wt. W2544/1454 700,000 5/15 D. D. & L. A.D.S.S./Forms/C. 2118.

Instructions regarding War Diaries and Intelligence Summaries are contained in F. S. Regs., Part II. and the Staff Manual respectively. Title pages will be prepared in manuscript.

No. 2.

WAR DIARY

or

~~INTELLIGENCE SUMMARY~~ of XI Mobile Vety Section by [signature] Capt AVC

(Erase heading not required.)

Army Form C. 2118.

Place	Date	Hour	Summary of Events and Information	Remarks and references to Appendices
BAPAUME	4.8.17.		on satisfactorily. 3 Susp. Mange cases admitted and washed in Calc. Sulp.	
"	5.8.17.		Fine. Four loads of corrugated iron and duck boards are drawn. Building of stables continued. Five susp. Mange cases are washed with Calc. Sulp. There are sixteen skin cases in the Section at present. O.C. proceeds on leave to U.K.	
"	6.8.17		Showery weather. Stable building continues. 4 Susp. Mange cases washed with Calc. Sulp. Four skin cases admitted. D.A. D.V.S. called this afternoon. 12 skin cases passed for evacuation.	
"	7.8.17.		Warm day follows a misty morning. 12 mange and 3 surgical cases were evacuated from BAPAUME to No 7 Veterinary Hospital. D.A. D.V.S. called. Further progress is made with building of SO_2 chamber. Turner Bibby Pad. put in for further trial. Two horses were washed in Calc. Sulp. Five gal. of Calc. Sulp. issued to 23 Batty.	
"	8.8.17		Fine. Good progress is being made with stables. Five horses sweated and scrubbed. Two skin cases returned to units cured.	
"	9.8.17.		Two Nissen Huts are drawn from HUN DUMP. Stable building continues. D.A. D.V.S. visited Section.	

2353 Wt. W2544/1454 700,000 5/15 D. D. & L. A.D.S.S./Forms/C. 2118.

Instructions regarding War Diaries and Intelligence Summaries are contained in F. S. Regs., Part II. and the Staff Manual respectively. Title pages will be prepared in manuscript.

No.3.

WAR DIARY
~~or~~
~~INTELLIGENCE SUMMARY.~~
(Erase heading not required.)

of XI Mobile Veterinary Section by [signature] Capt A.V.C.

Army Form C. 2118.

Place	Date	Hour	Summary of Events and Information	Remarks and references to Appendices
BAPAUME	10.8.17		Five animals that have been under treatment for Susp Mange were returned to their units cured. One suspected mange case is admitted. Two horses were redressed with Calc. Sulp. No 17649 Pte Isbell R reported for duty from No 7 Veterinary Hospital	
"	11.8.17		Stable and Hut building continues. Four horses suffering from Susp. Mange are admitted. Examination of scrapings taken from two horses from 45 Batty revealed the presence of Eggs. Five gals of Calc. Sulp. are issued to 41 Batty. 17154 Pte Wade J proceeded to No 1 Vety Hospital	
"	12.8.17		Fine. 3 horses were washed in Calc. Sulp today. Building of stable and huts proceeds. D.A.D.V.S called in the afternoon and inspected SO_2 Chamber and sick horses	
"	13.8.17		One susp Mange case admitted. One hut completed. Tar and pitch were drawn from HUN DUMP. Twenty seven sick horses were admitted.	
"	14.8.17		Fine. Cement was drawn for stable flooring. 27 sick and 3 mange evacuated from BAPAUME to No 7 Veterinary Hospital. One susp. Mange case admitted. D.A.D.V.S visited Section this afternoon.	
"	15.8.17		Two Susp Mange Cases that had been under treatment returned cured to their units.	

2353 Wt. W2544/1454 700,000 5/15 D. D. & L. A.D.S.S./Forms/C. 2118.

No. 4

Army Form C. 2118.

Instructions regarding War Diaries and Intelligence Summaries are contained in F. S. Regs., Part II. and the Staff Manual respectively. Title pages will be prepared in manuscript.

WAR DIARY of XI Mobile Veterinary Section
or
~~INTELLIGENCE~~ SUMMARY. by Capt. A.V.C.

(Erase heading not required.)

Place	Date	Hour	Summary of Events and Information	Remarks and references to Appendices
BAPAUME	15.8.17		A.D.V.S. IV Corps called and inspected SO_2 chamber. 5806 Pte NEWMAN F. reported for duty from No 3 Veterinary Hospital	
"	16.8.17		Several loads of bricks were drawn today and further progress made with the building of stables. 2 horses were washed with Calc. Sulp. and 3 horses sweated and scrubbed.	
"	17.8.17		13 Sick were evacuated from BAPAUME to No 7 Veterinary Hospital. 6381 Pte PENFRS. G proceeded to No 3 Veterinary Hospital. 1280 Pte Wheeler E. J. promoted P.A. Corporal to date from 16.7.17. O.C. returns from leave. Bricks are drawn for stables. One hut is occupied.	
"	18.8.17		Building of stables continued. Pharmacy is built. One horse dressed with Calc. Sulp.	
"	19.8.17		2 Cases of Susp Mange were admitted. Dressing shed is built. A second SO_2 Chamber is being built.	
"	20.8.17		Six Suspected mange cases and eighteen surgical were admitted. More Timber is drawn for stables. Section was paid at 6 p.m.	
"	21.8.17		24 Sick and 7 Susp Mange cases were evacuated to No 7 Veterinary Hospital from BAPAUME. A new cookhouse is being built. Second hut completed.	

2353 Wt. W2544/1454 700,000 5/15 D. D. & L. A.D.S.S./Forms/C. 2118.

Instructions regarding War Diaries and Intelligence Summaries are contained in F. S. Regs., Part II. and the Staff Manual respectively. Title pages will be prepared in manuscript.

No 5

WAR DIARY ~~or~~ INTELLIGENCE ~~SUMMARY~~.

of XI Mobile Vety Section by [signature] Capt A.V.C.

(Erase heading not required.)

Army Form C. 2118.

Place	Date	Hour	Summary of Events and Information	Remarks and references to Appendices
BAPAUME	22.8.17		Timber and corrugated iron are drawn. Two Nissen huts are tarred. Several loads of bricks are drawn for standings. Two susp. mange cases were admitted. Three horses were scrubbed and sweated. Stables are now completed for 40 horses.	
"	23.8.17		One susp mange case admitted. Bricks and saw-dust are drawn for standings. Two horses have been treated in the SO_2 chamber. Psoroptic Parasite found in mange scrapings.	
"	24.8.17		13 sick were evacuated from BAPAUME to No 7 Veterinary Hospital. Four horses were treated in the SO_2 chamber. T3/024388 Dr Morris H. admitted to Hospital. One susp mange case admitted.	
"	25.8.17		3 horses were treated in SO_2 chamber and 2 horses scrubbed. Ten loads of bricks were drawn. Forage barn and cook house tarred.	
"	26.8.17		Building of new stable for 60 horses is started. 2 susp mange cases admitted. 5 horses have been treated in SO_2 chamber today. 3 horses scrubbed & sweated.	
"	27.8.17		One susp mange case admitted. Five blow lamps drawn from R.E. Dump. Unusually heavy rain hinders work of stable building.	
"	28.8.17		8 sick and 2 mange were evacuated today to No 7 Veterinary Hospital from Bapaume. 2 horses under treatment for susp mange were returned cured to units.	

2353 Wt. W2544/1454 700,000 5/15 D. D. & L. A.D.S.S./Forms/C. 2118.

No 6

Instructions regarding War Diaries and Intelligence Summaries are contained in F. S. Regs., Part II. and the Staff Manual respectively. Title pages will be prepared in manuscript.

WAR DIARY

~~or~~

~~INTELLIGENCE SUMMARY.~~

(Erase heading not required.)

of ~~XI~~ Mobile Vety Section by [signature] Capt A.V.C.

Army Form C. 2118.

Place	Date	Hour	Summary of Events and Information	Remarks and references to Appendices
BAPAUME	28.8.17	2.p.m	Medical inspection of men at D.H.Q took place this afternoon.	
"	29.8.17		D.D.V.S. Third Army, visited section and inspected arrangements for horses and men. He expressed his satisfaction with the work done by the Section during the past six weeks. Five cases of susp. Mange were admitted. Four horses were treated in SO_2 chamber. 2 horses were sweated and scrubbed	
"	30.8.17		Progress made with stable building. Camp for mange horses wired round. Three horses were treated in $S.O_2$ chamber	
"	31.8.17		24 sick and 3 mange evacuated from BAPAUME to No 7 Veterinary Hospital. 2 Susp mange Cases discharged to units cured.	

[initials]

2353 Wt. W2544/1454 700,000 5/15 D. D. & L. A.D.S.S./Forms/C. 2118.

Instructions regarding War Diaries and Intelligence Summaries are contained in F. S. Regs., Part II. and the Staff Manual respectively. Title pages will be prepared in manuscript.

No. 1

WAR DIARY
or of XI Mobile Veterinary Section by
~~INTELLIGENCE SUMMARY.~~
(Erase heading not required.)

Army Form C. 2118.

Capt R.A.V.C.

Vol 38

Place	Date	Hour	Summary of Events and Information	Remarks and references to Appendices
BAPAUME	1.9.17		3 sick were admitted and one reissued today. 3 skin cases treated in SO_2 chamber. Material drawn for building Sergeants' Mess. Building of new stable continued.	
"	2.9.17		10 sick admitted and one reissued.	
"	3.9.17		32 sick admitted. D.A.D.V.S. called and inspected horses for evacuation and reissue. Stable building continued.	
"	4.9.17		38 sick were evacuated from BAPAUME to No 7 Veterinary Hospital. 3 horses were admitted and 5 reissued. 4 horses scrubbed.	
"	5.9.17		8 horses admitted and 6 reissued. One horse treated in SO_2 chamber.	
"	6.9.17		12 horses admitted and one reissued.	
"	7.9.17		5 horses admitted, 2 reissued and 17 evacuated from BAPAUME to 7 Veterinary Hospital	
"	8.9.17	11.45am	Section moved from BAPAUME	
ROCQUIGNY	8.9.17	2 p.m	Section arrived at ROCQUIGNY. Temporary quarters erected. D.A.D.V.S. called.	
"	9.9.17		Improvements to site carried out.	
"	10.9.17		7 sick admitted and 2 reissued. 2 Fumigating Chambers taken to site for M.V.S at LE MESNIL	
	11.9.17.		Four men go from Section to prepare M.V.S site at LE MESNIL. 2 lorries obtained to draw material. 2 sick admitted, 2 reissued and 9 evacuated from ROCQUIGNY to 7 Veterinary Hospital.	

2353 Wt. W2544/1454 700,000 5/15 D. D. & L. A.D.S.S./Forms/C. 2118.

Instructions regarding War Diaries and Intelligence Summaries are contained in F. S. Regs., Part II. and the Staff Manual respectively. Title pages will be prepared in manuscript.

No 2

WAR DIARY or ~~INTELLIGENCE SUMMARY~~. of XI Mobile Veterinary Section by [illegible] Capt AVC.

(Erase heading not required.)

Army Form C. 2118.

Place	Date	Hour	Summary of Events and Information	Remarks and references to Appendices
ROCQUIGNY	12.9.17		Work continued on new M.V.S. site. One sick admitted and 2 reissued	
"	13.9.17		One horse admitted and one reissued. Building on new site for M.V.S. continued	
"	14.9.17		One horse reissued and 3 sent to 1/1 London M.V.S for evacuation. Building of 2 Nissen huts @ LE MESNIL completed	
"	15.9.17	10.am	Section moved from ROCQUIGNY to BAPAUME arriving at 12 oc. Entrained at 2 p.m.	
HOPOUTRE	16.9.17	4.30am	Section detrained at HOPOUTRE and marched to WATOU.	
WATOU	16.9.17	8.30am	Section arrives at K10a68 Sheet 27.	
"	17.9.17		Site rather unsuitable for M.V.S.	
"	18.9.17		Better site sought for.	
"	19.9.17		1 Sick admitted	
"	20.9.17		Section moved from K10a6.8 to L5d8.7 Sheet 27. 3 Sick admitted	
"	21.9.17		Improvements to camp carried out.	
"	22.9.17		11 sick admitted and 1 reissued.	
"	23.9.17		2 Sick admitted.	
WATOU	24.9.17		Section moved at 10 a.m and arrived at	
POPERINGHE	24.9.17	12.p.m	3 Sick sent to Corps Mobile Vety Detachment. 9 Sick admitted. Advanced Dressing Station occupied.	

2353 Wt. W2544/1454 700,000 5/15 D. D. & L. A.D.S.S./Forms/C. 2118.

Army Form C. 2118.

No 3.

WAR DIARY or ~~INTELLIGENCE SUMMARY~~. of XI Mobile Vety Section by [illegible] Capt

(*Erase heading not required.*)

Instructions regarding War Diaries and Intelligence Summaries are contained in F. S. Regs., Part II. and the Staff Manual respectively. Title pages will be prepared in manuscript.

Place	Date	Hour	Summary of Events and Information	Remarks and references to Appendices
POPERINGHE	25.9.17		3 Sick admitted. 19 sick evacuated by road to 23 Veterinary Hospital	
"	26.9.17		13 Sick admitted. Three men detached from section for duty with Corps Mobile Vety Detachment	
"	27.9.17		7 Sick admitted	
"	28.9.17		8 Sick admitted. 10 sick sent to Corps Mobile Vety Detachment and 14 evacuated by road to 23 Veterinary Hospital	
"	29.9.17		14 Sick admitted. T2/14956 DR LATHAM C.A. A.S.C proceeded to Depot Field Survey for transfer to R.E	
	30.9.17		19 Sick admitted	

A5834 Wt. W4973/M687 750,000 8/16 D. D. & L. Ltd. Forms/C.2118/13.

I

Instructions regarding War Diaries and Intelligence Summaries are contained in F. S. Regs., Part II. and the Staff Manual respectively. Title pages will be prepared in manuscript.

WAR DIARY
or
~~INTELLIGENCE SUMMARY.~~ XIth Mobile Veterinary Section

(Erase heading not required.)

By. Hewell Capt. AVC. Commanding

Army Form C. 2118.

Vol 39

Place	Date	Hour	Summary of Events and Information	Remarks and references to Appendices
Sheet 28 G14.b.5.4	1-10-17	9 Am	Fine & warm, 43 Sick handed over to 3rd Australian M.V.S. for evacuation. Section moved to J18.b.4.4. Sheet 27. Started at 9 Am. arrived 12 noon	
Sheet 27 J18.b.4.4.	2-10-17		Fine & warm, 6 Sick admitted	
Do	3-10-17		Fine & warm, 9 Sick admitted	
Do	4-10-17	9 am.	15 Sick handed over to 66th Div. M.V.S. Section marched to RENESCURE at 9 Am. arriving @ 1 Pm. Heavy rain in the evening	
RENESCURE	5-10-17	10 A.m	Section moved to CONDARDENNE @ 10 A.M. arrived at 1 Pm.	
CONDARDENNE	6-10-17	2 A.M.	Section marched to WIZERNES @ 2 A.M. & entrained at 4 A.M. arrived @ BAPAUME @ 2.30 Pm. Men returned from V Corps Mobile Vety Detachment. Section marched to LE MESNIL arriving @ 5.20 Pm.	
LE MESNIL	7-10-17		2 Sick Admitted, Very heavy rain follows a particularly cold night. Improvements to horse standings & stabling commenced.	
Do	8-10-17		3 Sick Admitted, improvements to stabling continues. No S.E. 25202. Pte Bertles A. reports for duty from No 4 Vety Hospl. Very heavy rain in the evening.	
Do	9-10-17		No S.E. 1280 Sgt E. J. Wheeler proceeds to join 22 Hy Bty R.G.A. for duty. Improvements to Stabling carried on. Heavy rain all day. No 222141 L Cpl Wall J. 206 Employment Coy placed under close arrest for "Drunkenness"	
Do	10-10-17		1 Sick Animal admitted. S.E. 5085 Sgt F.A. KIERMAN. A.V.C. temporarily attached to Section awaiting orders, by order of D.A.D.V.S. Work of improving standings continues. Section & horse standings inspected by D.A.D.V.S. No 222141 L Cpl Wall J. 206 Employment Coy returned to his unit to await Field General Court Martial for "Drunkenness"	
Do	11-10-17		Work of improving horse standings continues No 124843 Pte Gardner W. 206 Employment Coy joins Section as loader.	

Instructions regarding War Diaries and Intelligence Summaries are contained in F. S. Regs., Part II. and the Staff Manual respectively. Title pages will be prepared in manuscript.

II

WAR DIARY or ~~INTELLIGENCE SUMMARY.~~

(Erase heading not required.)

By [signature] Capt. AVC Commanding XIst Mobile Vety Section

Army Form C. 2118.

Place	Date	Hour	Summary of Events and Information	Remarks and references to Appendices
LEMESNIL	12-10-17	9.30Am	7 Sick animals for evacuation hand over to 62nd Div M.V.S. Section moved to FAVREUIL at 9.30 Am arriving @ 12.45 Pm. 7 Sick Animals taken over from 62nd Div. M.V.S. No SE 29965 Pte Durbin A reports for duty from No 4 Vety Hospl. No 14649 Pte Isbell. R. returns from leave to U.K. Heavy rain all day.	
FAVREUIL	13-10-17		2 Sick animals admitted, No S.E. 5805 Sgt KIERMAN. F.W. A.V.C. proceed to join 2nd Div. D.A.C. 1 New horse ambulance drawn from R.O.O. Railhead BAPAUME. Work of improving horse standings commenced.	
"	14-10-17		2 Sick & 1 Ambulance case admitted No 13682 P/A/Corpl Kenny M. T. A.V.C proceeds to No 2 Vety Hospl for duty No 5205 Sgt Goodwin. W. & S.E. 3213 Sgt W.E. Smallridge. A.V.C ordered to attend Field General Court Martial on 222141 L. Cpl Wall. J. of 206 Employment Coy as witnesses. Work of improving Horse standings continues	
"	15-10-17		6 Sick animals admitted, 1 Destroyed, 17 Sick Evacuated to No 7 Vety Hospl. Timber & Corrugated Iron drawn from Engineers Dump for building of Stables etc, Building of Sgts Hut commences.	
"	16-10-17		2 Sick animals admitted, 1 Armstrong Hut drawn for Office & Qtr Mrs Store. Building of Sgts Hut & Stabling continues	
"	17-10-17		Building of Sgts Hut & Stables continues, 1 Armstrong hut erected	
"	18-10-17		4 Sick Admitted, Sgts Hut completed, S.E. 7657 Pte Rummery. H. proceed on leave to U.K. 19-10-17 to 29-10-17	
"	19-10-17		4 Sick Admitted, Building of Stabling & standings continues	
"	20-10-17		2 Sick animals admitted, Timber & tarred felt drawn for building Officers Mess & Cookhouse	

D. D. & L., London, E.C. (A8004) Wt W1771/M2031 750,000 5/17 Sch. 52 Forms/C2118/14

Instructions regarding War Diaries and Intelligence Summaries are contained in F. S. Regs., Part II. and the Staff Manual respectively. Title pages will be prepared in manuscript.

III

WAR DIARY
or
~~INTELLIGENCE~~ SUMMARY. XIth Mobile Veterinary Section

(Erase heading not required.)

Army Form C. 2118.

By Hewett. Capt. AVC Commanding

Place	Date	Hour	Summary of Events and Information	Remarks and references to Appendices
FAVREUIL	20-10-17	(Contd)	SE.22453. Pte Froggatt W.E. SE28858 Pte Gibney E. SE.30384. Pte Hall J. SE.1492 Hart C. SE.3426 Pte Hollis W. SE.24846 Mellor R. SE.25031 Pte ~~Mapnett~~ F.E. SE.30130 Pte Todd, A.W. SE.23010 Williams E.R. SE.20588. Pte Webster J. report for duty from No 6 Vety Hospl. Building of stabling continues	
"	21-10-17		Ptes SE.3039 Beale, W.S. SE.2043 Breitly R. SE.19259 Bushill J.R. SE3396 Crowley D. SE19259 Matthews C.J. SE5606 Newman F. SE.1423 Veal F.W. SE.2249 Warren E. proceed to No 2 Vety Hospl. 1 Sick & 1 Mange admitted, Officers mess & cookhouse completed. Section & standings inspected by G.O.C. 3rd Division. Building of stabling continues	
"	22-10-17		5 Sick animals admitted. Sick animals for evacuation inspected by D.A.D.V.S. Building of stabling continues	
"	23-10-17		15 Sick animals evacuated to No 4 Vety Hospl, 1 destroyed, Improvement of Horse Standings continues. SE.380 Pte Johns J. sustains a severely scalded face owing to camp kettle of (water boiling over.)	
"	24-10-17		2 Sick admitted improvements of standings continues.	
"	25-10-17		Ptes SE28858 Gibney E. & SE23010 Williams E.R. proceed to No I Vety Hospl for duty 17 Sick animals admitted. Section visited by D.A.D.V.S. Improvement of yard & horse standings continues	
"	26-10-17		19 Sick evacuated to No 4 Vety Hospl. Timber drawn from R.E. Dump for roofing stables. Dangerous structure pulled down under instructions of C.R.E. by order of Area Commandant 4 Sick animals admitted. SE.1492 Pte Hart C. admitted to Hospital. Heavy rain all day.	
	27-10-17		1 Sick animal admitted. Building of stables & standings continues.	
"	28-10-17		8 Sick animals admitted, building of stables & standings continues. SE1492 Pte Hart C. evacuated to No 9 C.C.S.	

D. D. & L., London, E.C. (A8004) Wt W1771/M2031 750,000 5/17 Sch. 52 Forms/C2118/14

Instructions regarding War Diaries and Intelligence Summaries are contained in F. S. Regs., Part II. and the Staff Manual respectively. Title pages will be prepared in manuscript.

IV

WAR DIARY or ~~INTELLIGENCE~~ SUMMARY.

(*Erase heading not required.*)

Army Form C. 2118.

XIth Mobile Veterinary Section

By. E Sewell. Capt. A.V.C. Commanding

Place	Date	Hour	Summary of Events and Information	Remarks and references to Appendices
FAVREUIL	29-10-17		7 Sick Animals admitted, 1 Destroyed, Animals for evacuation inspected by D.A.D.V.S. Dr Nash. L.A.S.C. (attd XI M.V.S) proceeds on leave to U.K. (30-10-17 to 9-11-17) Building of Stables & standings continues	
"	30-10-17		12 Sick evacuated to No 7 Vety Hospl, 2 Sick admitted. S.E. 880 Pte Johns J. admitted to Hospl. Improvements to Yard & standings continued	
"	31-10-17		6 Sick admitted, D.A.D.V.S. visits section, S.E. 20588 Pte. Webster J. proceeds on leave to U.K. leave granted from 1-11-17 to 15-11-17. Improvements to Yard & Stabling continues.	

D. D. & L., London, E.C. (A8004) Wt W1771/M2031 750,000 5/17 Sch. 52 Forms/C2118/14

I

WAR DIARY
or
~~INTELLIGENCE SUMMARY.~~
(Erase heading not required.)

Army Form C. 2118.

Instructions regarding War Diaries and Intelligence Summaries are contained in F. S. Regs., Part II. and the Staff Manual respectively. Title pages will be prepared in manuscript.

[signature] Capt. AVC
Commanding
XIth Mobile Veterinary Section

Vol 40

Place	Date	Hour	Summary of Events and Information	Remarks and references to Appendices
FAVREUIL	1/11/17		3 Sick Animals admitted, Timber drawn from R.E. Dump, for roofing of Stables. D.A.D.V.S visits Section & inspects Sick Animals for Evacuation.	
"	2/11/17		9 Sick Animals evacuated to No 4 Veterinary Hospital. 4 Sick Animals admitted, Improvements to stabling continued	
"	3/11/17		14 Sick Animals admitted, improvements to Stables continued	
"	4/11/17		3 Sick Animals admitted, S.E. 880 Pte Johns, J.F. rejoins Section for duty from No 3.C.C.S. Improvements to stabling continued	
"	5/11/17		12 Sick Animals admitted. D.A.D.V.S. Visits Section & inspects Sick Animals for Evacuation. Improvements to stables continues.	
"	6/11/17		22 Sick Animals evacuated to No 4 Veterinary Hospital. Improvements to stables continued	
"	7/11/17		1 Sick Animal admitted, D.A.D.V.S Visits section, Improvements to stables contd.	
"	8/11/17		Improvements to Stables continued.	
"	9/11/17		3 Sick animals admitted, Improvements to stables continued	
"	10/11/17		3 Sick Animals Admitted, 1 destroyed, Improvements to stables continued	
"	11/11/17		Section visited by D.A.D.V.S. Improvements continues	
"	12/11/17		O.C assumes duties of D.A.D.V.S during temporary absence of Major H. Greenfield granted leave to U.K. 21 Sick Animals admitted. Improvements continues	
"	13-11-17		28 Sick evacuated to No 4 Vety Hospital, 2 Sick Animals admitted. Improvements to Stables continued.	

D. D. & L., London, E.C.
(A8604) Wt W1771/M2031 750,000 5/17 Sch. 52 Forms/C2118/14

Instructions regarding War Diaries and Intelligence Summaries are contained in F. S. Regs., Part II. and the Staff Manual respectively. Title pages will be prepared in manuscript.

II

WAR DIARY
or
~~INTELLIGENCE SUMMARY.~~
(Erase heading not required.)

Army Form C. 2118.

[signature] Capt. AVC
Commanding
XIth Mobile Veterinary Section

Place	Date	Hour	Summary of Events and Information	Remarks and references to Appendices
FAVREUIL	14/11/17		5 Sick animals admitted, improvements to stables continued	
"	15/11/17		15 Sick animals admitted, improvements to stables continued	
"	16/11/17		14 Sick animals evacuated to 4 Vety Hospl. 3 Sick animals admitted, improvement to stables continued	
"	17/11/17		1 Sick animal admitted, 1 Barrel of Tar drawn from R.E. dump for tarring roofing of stables.	
"	18/11/17		1 Sick animal admitted, improvements to stables continues	
"	19/11/17		6 Sick & 3 Stray animals admitted. SE 20588 Pte Webster. J.H. returns from leave; improvements to stables continues.	
"	20/11/17		8 Sick animals evacuated to 4 Veterinary Hospital. 1 Sick animal admitted. SE 2043 Pte Brierly. R & SE. 10992 Pte Wells. G. report for duty from No 2 Vety Hospl.	
"	21/11/17		4 Sick animals admitted, improvements to stabling continues	
"	22/11/17		5 Sick animals admitted, SE. 3426 Pte Hollis. W. proceeds on leave to U.K. leave granted 23-11-17 to 7-12-17. Improvements to stabling continues.	
"	23/11/17		6 Sick animals evacuated to 4 Veterinary Hospital. SE. 20588 Pte Webster J.H. admitted to Hospital & evacuated to 49. C.C.S. C.O. reports sick, suffering from slipped knee. Improvements to stabled continues	
"	24/11/17		Improvements to stables continues.	
"	25/11/17		Timber & corrugated sheeting drawn from R.E. dump for building stable in Mange Camp.	

D. D. & L., London, E.C.
(A8004) Wt W1771/M2031 750,000 5/17 Sch. 52 Forms/C2118/14

Instructions regarding War Diaries and Intelligence Summaries are contained in F. S. Regs., Part II. and the Staff Manual respectively. Title pages will be prepared in manuscript.

III

WAR DIARY
or
INTELLIGENCE SUMMARY.
(*Erase heading not required.*)

Army Form C. 2118.

[signature] Capt. AVC
Commanding
XIth Mobile Veterinary Section

Place	Date	Hour	Summary of Events and Information	Remarks and references to Appendices
FAVEREUIL	26/11/17		4 Sick animals admitted. SE. 25031 Pte Mynett. F. E. A.V.C despatched to No2 Veterinary Hospital for duty, being surplus to War Establishment of M.V.S, Improvements to stables continues	
"	27/11/17		3 Sick animals admitted. Improvements of stabling continues	
"	28/11/17		1 H.D destroyed for Tetanus. D.A.D.V.S. returns from leave to U.K. Improvements to stabling continues	
"	29/11/17		3 sick animals admitted. D.A.D.V.S. visits section & inspects sick animals for evacuation. Improvements to stables continues	
"	30/11/17		8 Sick Animals sent to Railhead for evacuation & entrained. Owing to enemy shells falling in close proximity to Station, the R.T.O. ordered the animals to be detrained & removed to Section. 2 Sappers from 438 Fld Coy R.E attchd to Section & material drawn from R.E. Dump, for erecting ~~two~~ SO_2., Fumigating Chambers at M.V.S. Improvements to stables continued, 2 Sick animals admitted.	

D. D. & L., London, E.C.
(A8co4) Wt W1771/M2031 750,000 5/17 Sch. 52 Forms/C2118/14

No. 1

Army Form C. 2118.

Instructions regarding War Diaries and Intelligence Summaries are contained in F. S. Regs., Part II. and the Staff Manual respectively. Title pages will be prepared in manuscript.

WAR DIARY

~~or~~ of No. XI Mobile Vety Section

~~INTELLIGENCE SUMMARY.~~

(Erase heading not required.)

by Elwell Capt. AVC

Vol 41

Place	Date	Hour	Summary of Events and Information	Remarks and references to Appendices
FAVREUIL	1/12/17		4 Sick were admitted, building of 7. S.O. Chambers commences, 11 Sick Evac'd to 7th V.H.	
" "	2/12/17		1 Sick admitted, Building of S.O.s Chambers continues	
" "	3/12/17		22 Sick admitted, Building of S.O.s Chambers continues. D.A.D.V.S visits section and inspects animals for evacuation.	
" "	4/12/17		21 Sick Evac'd to 7. V.H, 4 Sick admitted. 10992 Pte Wells. G. admitted to Hospital. Building of S.O.s Chambers continue	
" "	5/12/17		9 Sick admitted, building of S.O.s Chambers continues	
" "	6/12/17		14 Sick admitted. D.A.D.V.S. visits sections, & inspects animals for evacuation, Building of S.O.s Chambers continues.	
" "	7/12/17		28 Sick evacuated to 7. V.H. 3 Sick & 1 Stray admitted, Building of S.O.s Chambers continues.	
" "	8/12/17		S.E. 1517 Pte Boyall W. awarded 1 days loss of pay, & 7 days C.G. for being absent from Conducting party. 3.15 AM to 11 AM 6/12/17. 7 Sick admitted. Building of S.O.s Chambers continues.	
" "	9/12/17		9 Remounts admitted to Section. Building of S.O.s Chambers continues.	
" "	10/12/17		5 Sick admitted Pte Hollis returns from leave to U.K. D.A.D.V.S. visits section & inspects horses for evacuation. Building of S.O.s Chambers continues	
" "	11/12/17		9 Sick evacuated to 7. Vety Hospital. A.D.V.S VI Corps visits section, & inspects Remounts and Cases with Eye trouble, & also inspects Stable & accomodation for N.C.O.s & men.	
" "	12/12/17		3 Sick admitted. Pte Froggatt proceeds on leave to U.K	
" "	13/12/17		3 Sick & 2 Strays admitted. D.A.D.V.S. inspects animals for evacuation.	
" "	14/12/17		7 Sick evacuated to 7th Vety Hospital [illegible]. 1 Sick admitted. 3213 P/A Sergt. Cmedbridge from P/A S Sergt L.E.O.73.	
" "	15/12/17		1 Animal destroyed. 2 Strays handed over to 37. M.V.S. Section moves to Ervillers @ 11 AM	
ERVILLERS	16/12/17		5 Sick admitted, improvement to standing Continues	
" "	17/12/17		1 Sick admitted, improvement to standing Continues. D.A.D.V.S Visits Section, inspects animals for evacuation	
" "	18/12/17		11 Sick admitted, 10 Sick, evacuated to 7. Vety Hospital	

D. D. & L., London, E.C.
(A8004) Wt W1771/M2031 750,000 5/17 Sch. 52 Forms/C2118/14

No 2.

WAR DIARY
~~or~~ of No. XI Mobile Vety. Section
~~INTELLIGENCE SUMMARY.~~
(Erase heading not required.)

G. Sewell Capt. AVC

Army Form C. 2118.

Instructions regarding War Diaries and Intelligence Summaries are contained in F. S. Regs., Part II. and the Staff Manual respectively. Title pages will be prepared in manuscript.

Place	Date	Hour	Summary of Events and Information	Remarks and references to Appendices
ERVILLERS	19/12/17		1 Sick animal admitted. S.E. 6916 Sergt. Lucas. G. A.V.C reports for duty from No 3 M.V.S.	
" "	20/12/17		S.E. 3313 Staff Sergt. Smallridge. W. A.V.C. proceeds to No 23 Vety. Hospital for duty. 5 Days of Hutting drawn (Quartering for Buildings) S.E. Pte Allum J. W. A.V.C. reported for duty from No 2 Vety. Hospital. D.A.D.V.S. inspects animals for evacuation	
" "	21/12/17		11 Sick evacuated to No 7 Vety. Hospital. 1 animal destroyed & 1 Sick admitted.	
" "	22/12/17		S.E. 25202 Pte Birtles. A. A.V.C admitted to Hospital. 5 Sick animals admitted. + S S Ross J. No 576 proceeds on leave to U.K	
" "	23/12/17		1 Sick animal admitted	
" "	24/12/17		S.E. No. 29348 Pte Cobb A. G. reported for duty from No 6 Vety. Hospital. 2 Sick animals admitted.	
" "	25/12/17		Pte Birtles. No. 25202 Sent to C.C.S. 5 Horses from Cheshire F. Coy R.E. injected with Lugol. Nothing to Report	
" "	26/12/17		1 animal admitted for issue. 115 G. I Sheets drawn for Building	
" "	27/12/17		16 Sick + 1 for issue admitted. building of Stable continues. D.A.D.V.S. Visits & inspects animals for evacuation. 1 animal destroyed	
" "	28/12/17		6 Sick animals admitted. and 23 evacuated to No 7 Vety. Hospital, including Brig. Gen. Tanner's Chargers (to be returned to owner) 1 mule from 233 M.G. Coy. injected with Lugol	
" "	29/12/17		5 Sick animals admitted. D.A.D.V.S Visits Section + inspects animals. 2 Horses 438 Cheshire F. Coy R.E. injected with Lugol. 1 Horse 6th Batty 40 Brigade injected with Lugol. 1 Horse 1st Roy. Scots Fus. injected with Lugol.	
" "	30/12/17		12 Horses from 129 Batty 42nd Brigade were injected with Lugol. Pte 7157. H. Rummery admitted to Hospital	
" "	31/12/17		10 Sick Horses admitted. D.A.D.V.S. Visits Section & inspects animals for evacuation. 8 Horses from 567 Coy. R.E. injected with Lugol 2 Horses 29th Batty 42 Bdge. injected Lugol 7 Horses from 45th Batty 42 Bdge injected with Lugol. 8 Horses from K.S.L.I injected with Lugol.	

D. D. & L., London, E.C.
(A8004) Wt W1771/M2031 750,000 5/17 Sch. 52 Forms/C2118/14

Instructions regarding War Diaries and Intelligence Summaries are contained in F. S. Regs., Part II. and the Staff Manual respectively. Title pages will be prepared in manuscript.

No I

WAR DIARY

or

~~**INTELLIGENCE SUMMARY.**~~

(Erase heading not required.)

of XI Mobile Veterinary Section by [illegible] Capt AVC

Army Form C. 2118.

Vol 42

Place	Date	Hour	Summary of Events and Information	Remarks and references to Appendices
ERVILLERS	1/1/18		14 Sick were evacuated to No 7 Vety Hospital including 8 mange. 2 Sick animals admitted	
"	2/1/18		1 Horse admitted for issue	
"	3/1/18		14 sick animals admitted + 1 destroyed No 7657 Pte RUMMERY transferred to Corps Rest Station	
	4/1/18		14 sick animals evacuated to No 7 Vety Hospital + 4 admitted to M.V.S.	
	5/1/18		1 H D issued to 20th K.R.R.C.	
	6/1/18		Two Horses returned to unit. Pte Jones proceeds on leave to U.K.	
	7/1/18		Six sick admitted. D.A.V.D.S. visits section + inspects animals for evacuation	
	8/1/18		Two sick admitted + Pte RUMMERY returned from rest station. 8 animals evacuated to No 7 Vet. Hospital Pte SPRINSTHORPE proceeds on leave to U.K.	
	9/1/18		Departure of Staff Sgt. Goodwin W to Havre.	
	10/1/18		Three sick admitted to section + S.S. Ross returned from leave to U.K.	
	11/1/18		Two Mange Horses evacuated to No 7 Vety Hospital	
	12/1/18		Two sick admitted + 5 injected with lugol	
	13/1/18		Three horses were injected with lugol + atropine	
	14/1/18		Eight sick admitted	
	15/1/18		Eight animals (6 horses 2 mules) evacuated to No 7 Vety Hospital. Horses paraded to A.D.V.S. office with Turner Bibby pads on. Pte No 72050 Innes W. reports for duty from 7/6 M.G.C. for training as Shoeing smith. 1 Horse injected with lugol + atropine 1 Horse admitted + issued the same day.	
	16/1/18		Two sick admitted + 2 horses injected with lugol.	

D. D. & L., London, E.C.
(A8005) Wt W1771/M2031 750,000 5/17 Sch. 52 Forms/C2118/14

Instructions regarding War Diaries and Intelligence Summaries are contained in F. S. Regs., Part II. and the Staff Manual respectively. Title pages will be prepared in manuscript.

Army Form C. 2118.

II WAR DIARY or ~~INTELLIGENCE SUMMARY.~~ of XI Mobile Vety Section by [illegible] Capt AVC.

(Erase heading not required.)

Place	Date	Hour	Summary of Events and Information	Remarks and references to Appendices
ERVILLERS	17.1.18		4 Sick admitted & SE No 21860 Pte Flanagan reports for duty from No 2 Vety Hospital	
			2 Horses injected with Lugol & Atropine	
	18/1/18		3 Sick admitted & S.E. No 29434 Pte Allen proceeds to No 2 Vety Hospital for duty & S.E. No 30310 Pte Todd A.W. proceeds on leave to U.K. 18/1/18 to 1/2/18.	
	19/1/18		3 Sick admitted	
	20/1/18		18 sick admitted & D.A.V.D.S. visits section & inspects animals for evacuation & 9 animals injected with Lugol.	
	21/1/18		22 Sick animal were evacuated to No 7 Vety Hospital & no sick admitted.	
	22/1/18		Staff Sgt Goodwin W. & Staff Sgt McDiamott Report to M.V.S.	
	23/1/18		2 Sick admitted & two horses injected with Lugol. L/Cpl Jones returns from leave to U.K.	
	24/1/18		2 Sick admitted & Pte Springthorpe returns from leave to U.K.	
	25/1/18		3 Sick admitted & 6 animals evacuated to No 7 Vety Hospital	
	26/1/18		SE No 7675 Pte Rummery admitted to Hospital	
	27/1/18		6 Sick admitted	
	28/1/18		The section marched from ERVILLERS to BOISLEUX-AU-MONT.	
BOISLEUX-AU-MONT	29/1/18		Pte Johns returned from leave to U.K. 24 sick admitted. DADVS visit section & inspects animals for evacuation	
"	30/1/18		44 Sick animals evacuated & 21 sick admitted. Staff Sgt Goodwin W. proceeds for duty to No 5 Vet Hospital	
	31/1/18		4 Sick admitted	

D. D. & L., London, E.C.
(A8c04) Wt W1771/M2031 750,000 5/17 Sch. 52 Forms/C2118/14

Instructions regarding War Diaries and Intelligence Summaries are contained in F. S. Regs., Part II. and the Staff Manual respectively. Title pages will be prepared in manuscript.

WAR DIARY or INTELLIGENCE SUMMARY.

XI Of II Mobile Veterinary Section

(Erase heading not required.)

Army Form C. 2118.

Vol 43

Place	Date	Hour	Summary of Events and Information	Remarks and references to Appendices
Boisleux.AU MONT.	Feb. 1		3 Sick animals admitted	
	2		Cpl Mumford W.K. proceeded on leave to U.K. one sick animal admitted	
	3		25 Sick animals admitted. D.A.D.V.S visited Section & inspected animals for evacuation.	
	4		Pte TODD. A.W. Returned from leave to U.K. & 32 sick animals were evacuated to No 7 Vety Hospital. 6 sick admitted	
	5		8 sick admitted & 2 discharged. Pte. Durbin. A. proceeded & leave to U.K. D.A.D.V.S visited section & inspected animals for evacuation	
	6		6 sick animals admitted & 16 evacuated to No 7 Vety Hospital. Cpl Knights proceeded to Havre for instruction in dressing to qualify as vety Sgt. to a field unit.	
	7		6 sick admitted. 1 destroyed. 11 evacuated to No 7 Vety Hospital Pte Mellor R. proceeded on leave to U.K.	
	8		6 sick animals were admitted.	
	9		3 sick animals admitted & Pte. Bruely R. proceeded on leave to U.K.	
	10		Ten sick animals were admitted. The D.A.D.V.S. inspected animals for evacuation	
	11		7 animals admitted & 23 evacuated to No 7 Vety Hospital	
	12		7 sick animals admitted & D.A.D.V.S. inspected animals for evacuation	
	13		1 sick admitted & 13 animals evacuated to No 7 Vety Hospital.	
	14		9 sick admitted & 2 Discharged. Capt. Sewell. E. proceeded on leave to U.K.	Sewell Capt AVC i/c XI M.V.S.
	15		4 sick animals admitted	
	16		8 sick animals admitted & No 30384 Pte Hall J. admitted into Hospital	
	17		No S.E. 1349 Pte Rooks. J. proceeded on leave to U.K.	
	18		4 sick animals were admitted	H. T. Dammone Capt AVC Act OC XI M.V.S

D. D. & L., London, E.C. (A8co4) Wt W1771/M2031 750,000 5/17 Sch. 52 Forms/C2118/14

Instructions regarding War Diaries and Intelligence Summaries are contained in F. S. Regs., Part II. and the Staff Manual respectively. Title pages will be prepared in manuscript.

Army Form C. 2118.

WAR DIARY
or
INTELLIGENCE SUMMARY.
(*Erase heading not required.*)

XI Mobile Veterinary Section

Place	Date	Hour	Summary of Events and Information	Remarks and references to Appendices
BOISLEUX	19		7 Sick animals admitted	
AU MONT.	20		3 Sick admitted Cpl. Mumford W. Returned from leave to U.K.	
	21		7 Sick admitted. No 30384 Pte Hall J. proceed on leave to U.K. Pte Durkin A. Returned from leave to U.K. Dvr Langford A report for duty from 3rd Divisional Train.	
	22.		Pte Egan. P. report for duty from No 2 Vety Hospital. 11 Evacuated to No 7 Vety Hospital	
	23.		9 Sick admitted & Pte Mellor R. returned from leave to U.K.	
	24		1 Sick admitted, & D.A.D.V.S. inspected animals for evacuation	
	25		1 Sick admitted & 10 evacuated to No 7 Vety Hospital	
	26		2 Sick animals admitted	
	27		8 Sick admitted	
	28		3 Sick animals admitted	

H. L. Tomanic.
Capt AVC
Acting O.C. XI M.V.S.

D. D. & L., London, E.C.
(A8004) Wt W1771/M2031 750,000 5/17 Sch. 52 Forms/C2118/14

24

1.

Army Form C. 2118.

Instructions regarding War Diaries and Intelligence Summaries are contained in F. S. Regs., Part II. and the Staff Manual respectively. Title pages will be prepared in manuscript.

WAR DIARY
or ~~INTELLIGENCE SUMMARY.~~
of XI Mobile Vety Section 3 Division

(Erase heading not required.)

Vol 44

Place	Date	Hour	Summary of Events and Information	Remarks and references to Appendices
BOISLEUX-AU-MONT	March 1		10 Sick animals admitted.	
	2		Capt SEWELL AVC returned from leave to U.K.	
	3		6 Sick animals admitted	
	4		4 Sick animals admitted	
	5		2 Sick animals admitted	
	6		9 Sick animals admitted & Pte ROOKS. T. AVC returned from leave to U.K.	
	7		7 Sick animals admitted.	
	8		D.A.D.V.S. visited Section to inspect horses for evacuation. 13 Evacuated to No 7 Vety Hosp. Pte Boyall W. proceeded on leave to UK 8.3.18 – 22.3.18	
	9		5 Sick animals admitted.	
	10		2 Sick animals admitted. Pte HALL J. AVC returned from leave to U.K.	
	11		Nothing to report.	
	12		5 Sick animals admitted & DADVS inspected horses for evacuation.	
	13		2 Sick animals admitted & 9 evacuated to No 7 Vety Hospital	
	14		4 Sick animals admitted & 2 discharged to 8th East Yorks transport.	
	15		Nothing to report. Field firing course on Rifle Range at MERCATEL begun	
	16		1 Sick animal admitted Field firing course on Range finished. Results good	Sewell. Capt AVC OC XI M.V.S.

D. D. & L., London, E.C. (A8004) Wt W1771/M2031 750,000 5/17 Sch. 52 Forms/C2118/14

2.

Army Form C. 2118.

Instructions regarding War Diaries and Intelligence Summaries are contained in F. S. Regs., Part II. and the Staff Manual respectively. Title pages will be prepared in manuscript.

WAR DIARY
or ~~INTELLIGENCE SUMMARY.~~ of XI Mobile Vety Section

(Erase heading not required.)

Place	Date	Hour	Summary of Events and Information	Remarks and references to Appendices
BOISLEUX-AU MONT	17.		6 Sick animals admitted.	
	18.		10 Sick animals evacuated to No 7 Vety Hosp. DADVS visited Section 6 Sick animals admitted. Capt TORRANCE AVC returned from leave to U.K.	
	19.		9 Sick horses & 6 Mules (Sick) admitted.	
	20.		D.A.D.V.S. visited Section to inspect sick. 20 animals evacuated to No 7 Vety Hosp.	
	21.		3 Sick animals admitted.	
GROSVILLE	22		Section shelled in morning. No SE 880 Pte JOHNS. T. wounded & evacuated to BASE. Moved Section to sunken road. Admitted & attended 9 horses belonging to R.A. H.Q. wounded by Shell fire. Section moved at 11 30 a.m from BOISLEUX-AU-MONT to GROSVILLE.	
	23.		11 Sick & Wounded Horses admitted.	
	24		1 Mule issued to 1st R.S.Fus. 1 Horse issued to 3rd M.G. Battn. 5 wounded horses admitted	
	25.		14 Wounded animals evacuated to No 5 Vety Hospl. 2 Horses & 1 Mule admitted	
	26		6 Remounts drawn from MONDICOURT. 2 Horses wounded by shell fire admitted. Major GREENFIELD A.V.C. D.A.D.V.S. 3rd Divn reported Sick. Assumed duties D.A.D.V.S. 3rd DIVISION	
	27		Nothing to record	

[signature] Capt A.V.C.
O.C. XI Mob Vety Sectn.

D. D. & L., London, E.C.
(A8004) Wt W1771/M2031 750,000 5/17 Sch. 52 Forms/C2118/14

3

Army Form C. 2118.

WAR DIARY
or
~~INTELLIGENCE~~ SUMMARY. of XI Mobile Vety Section

(Erase heading not required.)

Instructions regarding War Diaries and Intelligence Summaries are contained in F. S. Regs., Part II. and the Staff Manual respectively. Title pages will be prepared in manuscript.

[illegible] Capt. avc. [illegible]

Place	Date	Hour	Summary of Events and Information	Remarks and references to Appendices
GROSVILLE	March 28.		Section moved at short notice from GROSVILLE to GOUY-EN-ARTOIS Arrived new billets 5 p.m. Adv. Dressing Station left in GROSVILLE. Section was shelled about 2.30 p.m.	
GOUY-EN-ARTOIS	29.		12 Wounded animals admitted to Section. Adv. Dressing Station withdrawn	
LUCHEUX	30.		Section marched from GOUY-EN-ARTOIS to LUCHEUX at 9 a.m. 14 animals evacuated to No5 Vety. Hosp. from GOUY-EN-ARTOIS. Heavy rains.	
	31.		Nothing to record.	

D. D. & L., London, E.C.
(A8004) Wt W1771/M2031 750,000 5/17 Sch. 52 Forms/C2118/14

11

No. 1

3

Army Form C. 2118.

Instructions regarding War Diaries and Intelligence Summaries are contained in F. S. Regs., Part II. and the Staff Manual respectively. Title pages will be prepared in manuscript.

WAR DIARY
~~or~~
~~INTELLIGENCE SUMMARY.~~ of XI Mobile Vety Section

(Erase heading not required.)

E. Elwell Capt. AVC

Place	Date	Hour	Summary of Events and Information	Remarks and references to Appendices
AVERDOINGT	April 1		Section moved from LUCHEUX to AVERDOINGT.	WO 45
BRUAY.	2		Section moved from AVERDOINGT to BRUAY.	
	3		16 Remount & sick animals admitted.	
	4		14 Sick animals admitted.	
HESDIGNEUL.	5		Section moved from BRUAY to HESDIGNEUL. 6 Sick animals admitted.	
	6		A.D.V.S. inspected horses for evacuation 2 Sick animals admitted.	
	7		2 Sick animals admitted. 1 Animal for issue admitted. 16 Sick horses and 2 sick mules evacuated to No 23 Vety. Hospl.	
	8		8 Sick animals admitted.	
	9		2 Sick animals admitted.	
	10		1 Sick animal admitted.	
BUSNETTS.	11		Section moved from HESDIGNEUL to BUSNETTS.	
HURIONVILLE	12		Section moved from BUSNETTS to HURIONVILLE. 1 Sick animal admitted	
	13		2 Sick animals admitted. One sick animal destroyed	
	14		8 Sick animals evacuated to 23rd Vety: Hospl: 6 Sick animals admitted	
	15		6 Sick animals evacuated. Pte. TUCKER, L.E. reported for duty from No 15 Vety: Hospl	
BRUAY	16		Section moved from HURIONVILLE to BRUAY. 4 Sick animals admitted.	
	17		4 Sick animals admitted. 1 Sick animal destroyed and sold to M. DILLY LAURENT, 60 RUE du HAMEL, BRUAY. for 200 Francs (Two hundred fcs) 1 Sick animal died	E. Elwell Capt. AVC

D. D. & L., London, E.C.
(A8co4) Wt W1771/M2031 750,000 5/17 Sch. 52 Forms/C2118/14

No. 2.

Instructions regarding War Diaries and Intelligence Summaries are contained in F. S. Regs., Part II. and the Staff Manual respectively. Title pages will be prepared in manuscript.

WAR DIARY
~~or~~
~~INTELLIGENCE SUMMARY.~~ of XI Mobile Vety Section

by E. Sewell Capt. AVC.

(Erase heading not required.)

Army Form C. 2118.

Place	Date	Hour	Summary of Events and Information	Remarks and references to Appendices
BRUAY.	18		5 Stray animals and 1 sick animal admitted.	
	19		6 Stray and 2 sick animals admitted. 1 Sick animal evacuated	
	20		6 Ptes: detailed for duty at 1st Army Corps Veterinary Evacuation Station. 5 Sick animals admitted 13 Sick animals evacuated	
	21		Ptes BENNETT, H. BRYANT, and BUNCE reported for duty from No 14 Vety: Hospital. 14 Sick animals admitted. 3 Sick animals evacuated	
	22		2 Sick animals admitted, 2 Sick animals destroyed. 12 Animals evacuated. 2 Animals issued	
	23		No 834 Pte BENNETT, W. proceeded to No 2 Vety. Hosp: for duty. Six sick animals admitted. 5 Sick animals evacuated	
	24		5 Sick animals admitted 4 Sick animals evacuated.	
	25		3 Ptes returned from duty at 1st Corps Vety Evacuation Station. 7 Sick animals admitted 4 Sick animals evacuated.	
	26		2 Sick animals admitted, 11 Animals issued. Sergt Green detailed for duty at 9th Inf: Bde.	
	27		No T/35-362 Dr BLACKWELL, E. reports for duty from No 4 Coy. 3rd Divl Train and No T/508210 Dr GOUGH, L. reports for duty from No 7 Coy 3rd Divl Train. 2 Sick animals admitted 1 Sick anim died.	
BOIS DE DAMES	28		Section moved from BRUAY to BOIS de DAMES 2 Sick animals admitted	
	29		8 Sick animals admitted	
	30		12 Sick animals admitted 3 Animals for issue admitted 16 Sick animals evacuated 1 Animal destroyed This mobile section was formed on mobilization and proceeded over seas with 1914 Expeditionary Force	E. Sewell Capt A.V.C O.C. XI M.V.S.

D. D. & L., London, E.C. (A8c04) Wt W1771/M2031 750,000 5/17 Sch. 52 Forms/C2118/14

7 3

Army Form C. 2118.

No. I

WAR DIARY
or
INTELLIGENCE SUMMARY.
of II Mobile Vety Section by [illegible] Capt A.V.C

(Erase heading not required.)

Instructions regarding War Diaries and Intelligence Summaries are contained in F. S. Regs., Part II. and the Staff Manual respectively. Title pages will be prepared in manuscript.

Vol 4 6

Place	Date	Hour	Summary of Events and Information	Remarks and references to Appendices
BOIS DES DAMES	May 1		18 Sick animals admitted 1 Mule issued	
	2		D.A.D.V.S. inspects horses for evacuation. No. SE 1517 Pte BOYALL W. and No. SE 22753 Pte FROGGATT awarded 3 Extra Stable Guards for being absent off 2 o'clock parade, No. SE 29966 Pte DUBBINA awarded 7 Days Field Punishment No. 2 for (1) Being absent off 2 o'clock parade. (2) Ill treating a wounded horse. 3 Sick and 1 Stray animals admitted, 1 animal issued.	
	3		26 Sick animals evacuated to No. 13 Vety Hospital NEUFCHATEL. 14 Sick admitted.	
	4		14 Sick animals admitted, 5 Animals issued.	
	5		D.A.D.V.S. inspects animals for issue, 4 Animals issued, 22 Sick admitted.	
	6		6 Sick Animals admitted, 12 Animals issued, 2 Sick Destroyed. Sergt LUCAS Pte COLLINS detailed for duty at Advanced Dressing Station at CHOCQUES.	
	7		No. SE 6269 Sergt GREEN returned from temporary duty at 9th Inf Bde, No. 834 Pte BENNETT, W returned from Medical examination at No. 2 Vety Hospital, 12 Sick animals admitted, 40 Evacuated to No. 13 Vety Hospital, 1 Destroyed & 1 Issued.	
	8		6 Sick animals admitted.	
	9		14 Sick animals admitted, 1 animal issued.	

D. D. & L., London, E.C.
(A8004) Wt W1771/M2031 750,000 5/17 Sch. 52 Forms/C2118/14

Army Form C. 2118.

Instructions regarding War Diaries and Intelligence Summaries are contained in F. S. Regs., Part II. and the Staff Manual respectively. Title pages will be prepared in manuscript.

No II WAR DIARY
or ~~INTELLIGENCE SUMMARY.~~ Of XI Mobile Vety Section by [signature] Capt A.V.C.

(Erase heading not required.)

Place	Date	Hour	Summary of Events and Information	Remarks and references to Appendices
BOIS DES DAMES	May 10		3 Sick animals admitted, 3 Strays admitted, 17 Sick evacuated to No 13 Vety Hosp, 1 Destroyed & 1 Issued.	
	11		4 Sick animals admitted, 3 Animals issued, No 834 Pte BENNETT W and No S.E. Pte COBB A. were this day dispatched to No 2 Vety Hospital for duty, Sergt GREEN and Pte MELLOR sent to relieve Advanced Dressing Station at CHOCQUES	
	12		10 Sick animals admitted.	
	13		38 Sick animals admitted, 3 Destroyed, 5 Issued.	
	14		9 Sick admitted, 41 Evacuated to No 13 Vety Hosp.	
	15		7 Sick animals admitted, 1 Issued, Advance Dressing Station at CHOCQUES withdrawn.	
	16		6 Sick admitted, 4 Issued.	
	17		3 Sick and 8 Remounts for issue admitted, 14 Sick evacuated to No 13 Vety Hosp. 2 Issued.	
	18		15 Sick animals admitted, 4 Issued.	
	19		6 Privates A.V.C. detailed for duty at V.E.S. XIII Corps PERNES. 12 Sick animals admitted, 9 Animals issued. Assumed duties as D.A.D.V.S. 3rd Division for Major GREENFIELD who proceeded on leave to U.K. 1 Sick animal Destroyed, Pte GREEN 2nd Royal Scots reports for tempy duty at this section.	
	20		9 Sick animals admitted, 14 Sick evacuated to V.E.S. XIII Corps PERNES, 2 Issued.	
	21		7 Sick animals admitted, 9 Evacuated to V.E.S., 3 Issued.	
	22		8 Sick admitted, 9 Evacuated to V.E.S., 1 Issued.	
	23		9 Sick admitted, No T/508210 Dr GOUGH L. reports sick and is admitted to hospital via C.C.S.	

D. D. & L., London, E.C.
(A8004) Wt W1771/M2031 750,000 5/17 Sch. 52 Forms/C2118/14

Army Form C. 2118.

Instructions regarding War Diaries and Intelligence Summaries are contained in F. S. Regs., Part II. and the Staff Manual respectively. Title pages will be prepared in manuscript.

No. III WAR DIARY

or ~~INTELLIGENCE SUMMARY.~~ Of XI Mobile Vety Section by [illegible] Capt A.V.C.

(Erase heading not required.)

Place	Date	Hour	Summary of Events and Information	Remarks and references to Appendices
BOIS DES DAMES	May 24		No. 576 S/S ROSS, J. proceeds on one months leave to U.K., 5 Sick animals admitted, 12 Evacuated to V.E.S., 1 Issued.	
	25		8 Sick animals admitted, No. T/38812 Dr GARDNER J. A.S.C. reports for duty from No. 1 Coy 3rd Divl Train.	
	26		5 Sick animals admitted, 1 Issued, No. S.E. 33958 Pte EGAN, P. reports sick and is admitted to C.C.S.	
	27		9 Sick animals admitted, 11 Evacuated to V.E.S.	
	28		5 Sick animals admitted.	
	29		14 Sick animals admitted, 11 Evacuated to V.E.S.	
	30		4 Sick animals admitted, 14 Evacuated to V.E.S., 2 Issued, No. 206974 S/S DYKES, W. Royal Scots Fus. reported here for tempy. duty as S/S vice S/S ROSS, J. on leave.	
	31		One Sick horse admitted.	
				Capt A.V.C. O.C. XI Mob Vet Section

D. D. & L., London, E.C. (A8004) Wt W1771/M2031 750,000 5/17 Sch. 52 Forms/C2118/14

11 Mob V Sect 9

Instructions regarding War Diaries and Intelligence Summaries are contained in F. S. Regs., Part II. and the Staff Manual respectively. Title pages will be prepared in manuscript.

WAR DIARY for June 1918
or
~~INTELLIGENCE SUMMARY.~~
(*Erase heading not required.*)

by [signature] Capt A.V.C.
O.C. 11 Mobile Vety Section

Army Form C. 2118.

Vol 47

Place	Date	Hour	Summary of Events and Information	Remarks and references to Appendices
BOIS DES DAMES	June 1		No 690 S. Sergt McDIARMOTT, W. was this day dispatched to No 2 Vety. Hospital to reduce this section to new War Establishment. The G.O.C. 3rd Division visits section and expresses satisfaction with all arrangements. No SE. 5547 Pte SPRINGTHORPE, R. reports sick and is detained in hospital for observation. One sick horse admitted.	
	2		2 Sick animal admitted, 1 Issued.	
	3		4 Sick animals admitted.	
	4		2 Sick animals admitted. Pte SPRINGTHORPE R. returns to duty	
	5		3 Sick admitted, 12 Evacuated. No 11586 Royal Scots Pte IRONSIDE, W. reports for tempy. duty	
	6		7 Sick admitted, 1 Evacuated.	
	7		6 Sick admitted, 7 Evacuated, 4 Issued. Ptes GREEN and IRONSIDE return to 1st Royal Scots	
	8		7 Sick admitted, 2 Issued. Bombing protection for horse lines were this day completed	
	9		5 Sick admitted.	
	10		D.A.D.V.S. 3rd Division inspects sick for evacuation. 8 Sick admitted, 15 Evacuated, 2 Issued.	
	11		19 Sick animals admitted, 26 Evacuated.	
	12		1 Sick animal admitted, 1 Evacuated.	
	13		6 Sick animals admitted. Building of new cookhouse & mess room were this day completed	
	14		1 Sick animal admitted	
	15		5 Sick and 6 Remount animals admitted, 1 Sick Evacuated, 2 Issued.	

D. D. & L., London, E.C. (A8004) Wt W1771/M2031 750,000 5/17 Sch. 52 Forms/C2118/14

2

Instructions regarding War Diaries and Intelligence Summaries are contained in F. S. Regs., Part II. and the Staff Manual respectively. Title pages will be prepared in manuscript.

WAR DIARY *or* INTELLIGENCE SUMMARY.

for June 1918

(*Erase heading not required.*)

[illegible] Capt A.V.C. – O.C. XI Mobile Vety Section

Army Form C. 2118.

Place	Date	Hour	Summary of Events and Information	Remarks and references to Appendices
BOIS DES DAMES	16		1 Sick animal admitted.	
	17		7 Sick animals admitted. D.A.D.V.S. 3rd Divn inspects section, men and horses and is satisfied with all arrangements.	
	18		9 Sick animals admitted, 17 Evacuated, 7 Issued.	
	19		4 Sick animals admitted, 16 Evacuated, 1 Issued.	
	20		3 Sick animals admitted.	
	21		3 Sick animals admitted, 1 Evacuated. No SE 30296 Pte DUCKWORTH, J. A.V.C. reports for duty from No 2 Vety: Hospital.	
	22		A.D.V.S. XIII th Corps inspects section men & horses and expresses [illegible] satisfaction with all arrangements, 1 Sick horse admitted.	
	23		2 Sick animals admitted.	
	24		4 Sick animals admitted, 10 Evacuated, 1 Issued.	
	25		8 Sick animals admitted.	
	26		4 Sick animals admitted. Pte BREWSTER, G. 20th K.R.R. reports for tempy. duty with sick horses.	
	27		5 Sick animals admitted, 12 Evacuated, 2 Returned to units. No 576 S/S Ross J. returns from one months leave to U.K.	

D. D. & L., London, E.C.
(A8co4) Wt W1771/M2031 750,000 5/17 Sch. 52 Forms/C2118/14

3

Army Form C. 2118.

Instructions regarding War Diaries and Intelligence Summaries are contained in F. S. Regs., Part II. and the Staff Manual respectively. Title pages will be prepared in manuscript.

WAR DIARY for June 1918 by [illegible] Capt A.V.C. O.C. XI M.V.S.
or
~~INTELLIGENCE SUMMARY.~~
(Erase heading not required.)

Place	Date	Hour	Summary of Events and Information	Remarks and references to Appendices
BOIS DES DAMES	June 28		2 Sick horses admitted, 4 Sick animals Evacuated, 1 Returned to unit. Pte BREWSTER G. 20th H.R.R. returns to his unit.	
	29		7 Sick animals admitted, 1 Sick horse destroyed.	
	30		4 Sick animals admitted.	

[illegible] Capt A. V. C.
O. C. XI Mob. Vet. Sect.

D. D. & L., London, E.C.
(A8004) Wt W1771/M2031 750,000 5/17 Sch. 52 Forms/C2118/14

7 I 3

Instructions regarding War Diaries and Intelligence Summaries are contained in F. S. Regs., Part II. and the Staff Manual respectively. Title pages will be prepared in manuscript.

WAR DIARY
or
INTELLIGENCE SUMMARY.
(*Erase heading not required.*)

July 1918 by [signature] Capt A.V.C. O.C. XI Mob. Vet. Sect.

Army Form C. 2118.

Place	Date	Hour	Summary of Events and Information	Remarks and references to Appendices
BOIS DES DAMES	July 1		4 Sick animals admitted, 1 Returned to unit, 1 Evacuated.	
	2		3 Sick animals admitted, 1 Retd to unit, 13 Evacuated	
	3		2 Sick animals admitted.	
	4		1 Sick animal admitted	
	5		D.D.V.S. 5th Army inspects section and men and expresses satisfaction with all arrangments. 1 Sick animal Evacuated.	
	6		3 Sick animals admitted.	
	7		1 Sick animal admitted.	
	8		2 Sick animals admitted, 9 Evacuated. No SE 659 Pte RANBERT, T. proceeds on leave to PARIS 9-7-18 to 17-7-18. No SE 6269 Sergt GREEN G is detailed for duty with Remount Conducting Party & proceeds to BOULOGNE with same	
	9		No SE 15951 Pte COLLINS, B. & No SE. 20843 Pte BRYANT, S. report sick and are detained in hospital. 1 Sick horse admitted.	
	10		1 Sick mule Evacuated.	
	11		2 Sick Animals admitted. Sergt GREEN G. returns with Remount Conducting Party.	
	12		3 Sick Animals admitted.	
	13		3 Sick animals admitted, 5 Evacuated, 1 Issued. Pte COLLINS returns from hospital	

VDI 48

D. D. & L., London, E.C. (A8004) Wt. W1771/M2031 750,000 5/17 Sch. 52 Forms/C2118/14

II

Instructions regarding War Diaries and Intelligence Summaries are contained in F. S. Regs., Part II. and the Staff Manual, respectively. Title pages will be prepared in manuscript.

WAR DIARY for July 1918
or
INTELLIGENCE SUMMARY.
(Erase heading not required.)

Army Form C. 2118.

[signature] Capt
O.C. XI Mob. Vet. Sect.

Place	Date	Hour	Summary of Events and Information	Remarks and references to Appendices
BOIS DES DAMES	July 14		2 Sick mules admitted.	
	15		3 Sick animals admitted, 1 Evacuated, 1 Returned to unit. Pte BRYANT, S. returns from hospital.	
	16		13 Sick horses admitted. No T/32162 Dr GARDNER J. A.S.C. injures a finger of the right hand, reports sick & is excused duty.	
	17		3 Sick animals admitted 21 Evacuated. No SE. 30296 Pte DUCKWORTH reports sick and is admitted to hospital	
	18		16 Animals admitted, Dr GARDNER is admitted to hospital with ruptured tendon of finger	
	19		5 Sick animals admitted, 1 Died, Pte PATERSON 2nd Royal Scots reports here for duty with sick horses	
	20		1 Sick animal admitted 11 Evacuated.	
	21		1 Sick horse admitted, Pte RANGER, T. returns from leave to PARIS.	
	22		9 Sick animals admitted Pte DUCKWORTH J. returns from hospital.	
	23		6 Sick animals admitted, 10 Evacuated, 1 Returned to unit. No SE. 1517 Pte Boyan, W. awarded 7 days F.P. No II for "When on Active Service" I Neglect of Duty II Cruelty to a horse Government Property.	
	24		6 Sick animals admitted Dr GARDNER, J. returns from hospital.	

D. D. & L., London, E.C.
(A8004) Wt W1771/M2031 750,000 5/17 Sch. 52 Forms/C2118/14

III

Instructions regarding War Diaries and Intelligence Summaries are contained in F. S. Regs., Part II. and the Staff Manual respectively. Title pages will be prepared in manuscript.

WAR DIARY for July 1918
or
INTELLIGENCE SUMMARY.
(*Erase heading not required.*)

Army Form C. 2118.

[signature] Capt A.V.C. O.C. XI Mobile Vety. Section

Place	Date	Hour	Summary of Events and Information	Remarks and references to Appendices
BOIS DES DAMES	25		15 Sick animals admitted, 12 Evacuated, 1 Issued.	
	26		4 Sick animals admitted,	
	27		2 Sick Horses admitted	
	28		No SE 6269 Sgt GREEN G. proceeds on leave to U.K. 29/7/18 to 11/8/18. 2 Sick animals admitted	
	29		7 Sick animals admitted, 9 Evacuated	
	30		2 Sick ~~animals~~ admitted, 1 Rider issued.	
	31		3 Sick animals admitted, 1 Destroyed. 1 Died	

[signature] Capt A.V.C. O.C. XI M.V.S.

13 I 3

Instructions regarding War Diaries and Intelligence Summaries are contained in F. S. Regs., Part II. and the Staff Manual respectively. Title pages will be prepared in manuscript.

WAR DIARY
or
~~INTELLIGENCE SUMMARY.~~
(Erase heading not required.)

for August 1918 XI Mot. Vety Sect. Army Form C. 2118.

[signature] Capt A.V.C. O.C. XI Mot Vety Sect

Place	Date	Hour	Summary of Events and Information	Remarks and references to Appendices
BOIS DES DAMES	August 1-1918		1 Stray Mule Admitted	VR 49
	2		7 Sick animals evacuated to XIII V.E.S.	
	3		Nothing to report	
	4		D.D.V.S 5th Army Inspects Section and expresses satisfaction with all arrangements. 1 Sick animal admitted. T/S DYKES, W. Royal Scots Fus returns to his unit	
	5		7 Sick animals admitted	
	6		10 Sick animals evacuated to XIII V.E.S. Pte PATERSON D. 2nd Royal Scots returns to his unit	
RAIMBERT	7		Section moved from BOIS DES DAMES at 9 am. and arrived at new billet RAIMBERT at 11·30 am.	
	8		6 Sick animals admitted, 3 Evacuated to XIII V.E.S.	
	9		8 Sick animals admitted, 4 Evacuated to XIII V.E.S.	
AUCHEL	10		Section moved from RAIMBERT to AUCHEL and arrived at new billet at 1 PM. 1 Sick horse admitted. 5 Sick animals evacuated to XIII V.E.S.	
	11		2 Remount Horses received from 5th Army Remounts	

D. D. & L., London, E.C. (A8004) Wt W1771/M2031 750,000 5/17 Sch. 52 Forms/C2118/14

II

Instructions regarding War Diaries and Intelligence Summaries are contained in F. S. Regs., Part II. and the Staff Manual respectively. Title pages will be prepared in manuscript.

WAR DIARY for August 1918 XI Mob Vety Sect
or
~~INTELLIGENCE SUMMARY.~~
(Erase heading not required.)

by [signature] Capt A.V.C. O.C. XI Mob Vety Sec

Army Form C. 2118.

Place	Date	Hour	Summary of Events and Information	Remarks and references to Appendices
AUCHEL	August 12		Nothing to report	
ANVIN	13		Section moved from AUCHEL and arrived at ANVIN at 9 P.M. No S/E 833 Cpl JONES, A. proceeds on 14 days special leave to United Kingdom, 13/8/18 to 26/8/18	
HUMBERCOURT	14		Section moved from ANVIN at 7.30 P.M. and arrived at HUMBERCOURT at 5 am. the morning of the 15th inst.	
BAVINCOURT	15		Arrived at HUMBERCOURT. Section moved from HUMBERCOURT at 12 noon and arrived at BAVINCOURT at 2.30 P.M.	
	16		Section moved to new billets and arrived at 9.30 am 2 Sick animals admitted. Sergt GREEN, G returns from leave to United Kingdom. No S/E 33958 Pte EGAN, P reports for duty from No II Vety Hospl. to release No S/E 3771 Cpl MUMFORD, W for medical examination	
	17		4 Sick animals admitted. 1 Horse issued	
	18		No S/E 10992 Pte WELLS, G. Proceeds on 14 days leave to United Kingdom 19/8/18 to 1/9/18. 1 Sick animal admitted 7 sick evacuated to No VI V.E.S. 2 Remounts issued	
	19		No S/E 3771 Cpl MUMFORD, W. proceeds to No II Vety Hospl for medical examination for transfer to infantry as per instruction from D.V.S. No S/E 22622 U/A/L/Cpl TUCKER, L.E. appointed U/A/Cpl pending notice of transfer of Cpl MUMFORD to infantry or otherwise. 5 Sick animals admitted 4 Sick evacuated to No VI V.E.S.	

D. D. & L., London, E.C.
(A8004) Wt W1771/M2031 750,000 5/17 Sch. 52 Forms/C2118/14

III

Instructions regarding War Diaries and Intelligence Summaries are contained in F. S. Regs., Part II. and the Staff Manual respectively. Title pages will be prepared in manuscript.

WAR DIARY by
or
INTELLIGENCE SUMMARY.
(Erase heading not required.)

[illegible] for August 1918 Army Form C. 2118.
XI Mobile Vety Sect
Capt A.V.C,
O.C. XI Mob: Vety Section

Place	Date	Hour	Summary of Events and Information	Remarks and references to Appendices
LACAUCHIE	20		Section moved from BAVINCOURT at 9 am. and arrived new billet at LACAUCHIE at 10 am. Advanced Dressing Station established at MONCHY AU BOIS. 1 Sick Horse died Colic	
	21		1 Sick Horse admitted	
	22		13 Sick animals admitted 6 Evacuated to No VI V.E.S. Director General of Veterinary Services visits Advanced Dressing Station and Section.	
MONCHY AU BOIS	23		9 Sick animals admitted. 9 Sick evacuated to No VI V.E.S. 1 Sick horse died (Rupture of diaphragm. Section moved at 11.30 P.m. to MONCHY AU BOIS arriving new billet at 1.30 am. the morning of the 24th inst. Advanced Dressing Station established at DOUCHY	
	24		5 Sick animals admitted, 6 Sick evacuated to No VI V.E.S., 1 Sick horse handed to No III Mobile Vety Section at HUMBERCAMPS. 4 Remount mules received from Remount Section. 1 Horse for issue received from 2nd Divl H.Q.	
	25		9 Sick animals admitted, 7 Sick evacuated to No VI Vety Evac: Station. 2 Remount mules issued to 20th. K.R.R.C. 1 Horse from D.H.Q issued	
	26		12 Sick animals admitted 11 Sick evacuated to No VI V.E.S. [redacted]	
	27		7 Sick animals admitted	

D. D & L., London, E.C.
(A8004) Wt W1771/M2031 750,000 5/17 Sch. 52 Forms/C2118/14

IV

Army Form C. 2118.

Instructions regarding War Diaries and Intelligence Summaries are contained in F. S. Regs., Part II. and the Staff Manual respectively. Title pages will be prepared in manuscript.

WAR DIARY
or
~~INTELLIGENCE SUMMARY.~~
(*Erase heading not required.*)

for August 1918
Capt A.V.C
O.C. XI Mob. Vety. Sect.

Place	Date	Hour	Summary of Events and Information	Remarks and references to Appendices
BOIRY St RICTRUDE	28		Advanced Dressing Station withdrawn from DOUCHY and section moved at 9 a.m. and arrived at new billet at BOIRY St RICTRUDE at 2 pm. 1 sick horse admitted 13 sick animals evacuated to No VI V.E.S.	
	29		Advanced Dressing Station Established at HAMLINCOURT. No 3/E 21843 Pte FLANAGAN, R. appointed U/A/Cpl. 2 sick animals admitted	
	30		15 sick animals admitted. 1 Horse destroyed (P.U.N.) No 3/E 6796 Sergt LUCAS. G proceeds on 14 days leave to United Kingdom 31/8/18 to 13/9/18. D.D.V.S. 3rd Army inspects the section	
	31		3 Stray horses admitted 17 sick animals evacuated to No XVII V.E.S.	

D. D. & L., London, E.C.
(A8004) Wt W1771/M2031 750,000 5/17 Sch. 52 Forms/C2118/14

14 No. 1 3

Army Form C. 2118.

Instructions regarding War Diaries and Intelligence Summaries are contained in F. S. Regs., Part II. and the Staff Manual respectively. Title pages will be prepared in manuscript.

WAR DIARY for September 1918 or ~~INTELLIGENCE SUMMARY.~~

(Erase heading not required.)

by [signature] Capt A.V.C. O.C. XI Mobile Vety Sect. 11th MVS

Place	Date	Hour	Summary of Events and Information	Remarks and references to Appendices
BOIRY St. RICTUDE	Sept 1918 1st.		3 Sick animals admitted	50
	2nd.		9 Sick animals admitted. 3 Stray horses issued. 1 Horse returned to unit cured.	
	3rd.		3 men report for temporary duty from 3rd D. A. C. 2 Sick horses admitted. 1 Horse returned to unit cured. One sick horse suffering from wounds destroyed. Cpl MUMFORD, W. returns from medical examination at HAVRE	
	4th.		3 Sick animals admitted 11 Sick evacuated to No. VI V.E.S. 1 Horse issued. 1 Horse rec'd from VI V.E.S. for issue.	
	5th.		3 Sick animals admitted. 6 Sick evacuated to No. VI V.E.S. 1 Horse issued to 1st North. Fus.	
	6th.		1 Horse issued to 3rd Divn. M. G. Batn. 1 Sick horse admitted	
DOUCHY	7th.		Section moved at 1-30 P.M. and arrived new billets at DOUCHY at 4 P.M. 4 Sick horses admitted	
	8th.		Building of cookhouse started 11 Sick animals admitted	
	9th.		Building of cookhouse completed. 13 Sick animals admitted. No. S.E. 833 Cpl. JONES. A. returns from leave to U. K. 16 Sick animals evacuated to No. VI V. E. S. 2 Sick returned to units cured 3 Horses issued.	
	10th.		2 Stray Animals admitted. 7 Sick animals evacuated to No VI V. E. S. 3 Horses issued.	
	11th.		1 Sick animal admitted. 1 Evacuated by float to No. VI V. E. S.	

D. D. & L., London, E.C. (A8004) Wt. W1771/M2031 750,000 5/17 Sch. 52 Forms/C2118/14

11/5. 2

Instructions regarding War Diaries and Intelligence Summaries are contained in F. S. Regs., Part II. and the Staff Manual respectively. Title pages will be prepared in manuscript.

WAR DIARY
or
~~INTELLIGENCE SUMMARY.~~
(*Erase heading not required.*)

Army Form C. 2118.

Place	Date Sept 1918	Hour	Summary of Events and Information	Remarks and references to Appendices
DOUCHY	12th		Section moved at 9.30am from DOUCHY and arrived at new billets at ERVILLERS at 12.30P.M.	
ERVILLERS.	13th.		Considerable improvements made to existing stables at new billets. 3 Men returned to 3rd D. A. C.	
	14th		D. D. V. S. 3rd Army calls and inspects section. 1 Stray mule admitted	
VRAUCOURT	15th.		Section moved at 9.30 am. to VRAUCOURT and arrived new billets at 12 noon. Capt E. SEWELL proceeds on eight days leave to PARIS, 15/9/18 to 22/9/18	
VAULX-VRAUCOURT	16th.		Section moved from VRAUCOURT at 2.30 p.m and arrived new billet in sunken road at VAULX-VRAUCOURT at 3.30 pm. Stray mule claimed by 3rd M. G. Batn. 6 Sick animals admitted. 1 Stray mule admitted. No. S/E 6196 Sergt LUCAS, G. returns from leave.	
	17th.		Section moved from sunken road to ruined farm where good stabling had been found. 4 Sick mules admitted.	
	18th.		No. S/E 28929 Pte. GRIFFITHS, G. reports this unit for duty from No II Vety Hospl. 4 Sick animals admitted, 2 Floated.	
	19th.		2 Sick horse admitted, 1 Floated, 1 Sick horse destroyed suffering from Shell Wounds	
	20th.		17 Sick animals admitted from Corps units. 2 Floated. 27 Sick animals evacuated to No VI V.E.S	

D. D. & L., London, E.C.
(A8004) Wt W1771/M2031 750,000 5/17 Sch. 52 Forms/C2118/14

No. 8

Instructions regarding War Diaries and Intelligence Summaries are contained in F. S. Regs., Part II. and the Staff Manual respectively. Title pages will be prepared in manuscript.

WAR DIARY for September 1918
or
INTELLIGENCE SUMMARY. by
(*Erase heading not required.*)

Army Form C. 2118.

Capt A.V.C.
O.C. No. XI Mobile Vety Section

Place	Date Sept 1918	Hour	Summary of Events and Information	Remarks and references to Appendices
VAULX-VRAUCOURT	20th.		Motor Horse Ambulance obtained from VI Corps for the day to assist in evacuation work and four animals evacuated by it and two by float.	
	21st.		9 Sick animals admitted, 1 Sick horse evacuated to No VI V.E.S. by float. 1 Sick horse destroyed suffering from shell Wounds. A.D.V.S. VI Corps calls & inspects section.	
	22nd.		Capt E. SEWELL returns from leave to PARIS. 17 Sick animals admitted. 2 Returned to units cured. Part of stabling handed over to No. VI V.E.S.	
	23rd.		8 Sick animals admitted. 1 Horse & 1 Mule destroyed suffering from shell wounds. 2 Horses returned to units cured.	
	24th.		8 Sick animals admitted 29 Evacuated to No. VI V.E.S. 2 Horses destroyed suffering from shell wounds. No. S.E. 1517 Pte BOYALL W. awarded 21 days F.P. No. I for "When on Active Service Wilful destruction of Government Property.	
	25th.		10 Sick animals admitted. 8 Evacuated to No. VI V.E.S. 1 Horse destroyed suffering from Shell Wounds. Advanced Aid Post established at J 34 D and Collecting Station at LEBUCQUIERE	
LEBUCQUIERE	26th.		Section moved to LEBUCQUIERE at 9 a.m. Billet at VRAUCOURT being handed over to No. VI V.E.S. 4 Sick animals admitted. 1 Horse evacuated to No. VI V.E.S. by float.	

D. D. & L., London, E.C.
(A8004) Wt W1771/M2031 750,000 5/17 Sch. 52 Forms/C2118/14

No. 4.

Army Form C. 2118.

WAR DIARY for September 1918
or
~~INTELLIGENCE SUMMARY.~~
(Erase heading not required.)

by [signature] Capt A.V.C.
O.C. XI Mobile Vety Sect.

Instructions regarding War Diaries and Intelligence Summaries are contained in F. S. Regs., Part II. and the Staff Manual respectively. Title pages will be prepared in manuscript.

Place	Date	Hour	Summary of Events and Information	Remarks and references to Appendices
LEBUCQUIERE	27th		Number of Shells fell in vicinity of section and one horse killed. Section moved to sunken road at 9 am. 14 Sick animals admitted. 1 Sick horse destroyed suffering from lacerated wounds.	
	28th		9 Sick animals admitted, 2 by float. 16 Sick evacuated to No. VI V.E.S. 3 Floated.	
	29th		36 Sick animals admitted 12 Sick evacuated to No. VI V.E.S. 1 Horse destroyed suffering from Bomb Wounds	
	30th		4 Sick animals admitted 5 L.D. Horses received from No. VI V.E.S. for issue. 36 Sick evacuated to No VI V.E.S. 2 L.D. Horses issued to 2 nd Suffolks. Pte DUCKWORTH J. reports sick and is admitted to hospital suffering from poisoned hand.	

[signature] Capt A.V.C.
O.C. No XI Mob. Vety Sect.

D. D & L., London, E.C.
(A8604) Wt W1771/M2031 750,000 5/17 Sch. 52 Forms/C2118/14

13

Instructions regarding War Diaries and Intelligence Summaries are contained in F. S. Regs., Part II. and the Staff Manual respectively. Title pages will be prepared in manuscript.

WAR DIARY or INTELLIGENCE SUMMARY.

(Erase heading not required.)

Army Form C. 2118.

Capt A.V.C.
O.C. XI Mob. Vety. Sect.

Vol 52

Place	Date Oct 1918	Hour	Summary of Events and Information	Remarks and references to Appendices
HERMIES.	1		Section moved from LEBUCQUIERE to HERMIES. 1 Sick horse admitted	
	2		Nothing to report	
HAVRINCOURT	3		Dr GARDNER A.S.C. proceeds on 14 days leave to U.K. 4/10/18 to 18/10/18. Section moved from HERMIES to site on HAVRINCOURT-RIBECOURT road. Advanced aid post established at MARCOING. 9 L.D. Horses issued to 1st Gordons. 25 Sick animals admitted. 1 Floated	
	4		37 Sick animals admitted + 36 Evacuated to VI V.E.S. 1 Case Floated. 1 L.D. horse was destroyed on the road to Evacuation Station. 1 Horse returned to unit cured. 2 Mules issued to 129 Baty R.F.A.	
	5		15 Sick animals admitted + 22 Evacuated to VI V.E.S.	
	6		9 Sick animals admitted + 14 Evacuated to VI V.E.S. 1 L.D horse issued to 45th Baty R.F.A.	
	7		16 Sick animals admitted, 3 Cases Floated, 1 L.D. horse destroyed suffering from Lacerated Wounds	
	8		8 Sick animals admitted + 23 Evacuated to VI V.E.S. 1 Case by float. 1 H.D. horse issued to No III Coy 2nd Divl Train	
HERMIES.	9		Section moved from HAVRINCOURT-RIBECOURT road at 9.30 am. and arrived at new site in sunken road near The Slag Heap at HERMIES at 11.30 am. 1 Sick horse admitted. 7 Sick animals evacuated to VI V.E.S. 1 H.D. horse died suffering from Calculus.	
	10		No S/E 659 Pte RANGER T. proceeds on 14 days leave to U.K. 10/10/18 to 23/10/18. 6 Sick animals admitted	

D. D & L., London, E.C.
(A8004) Wt W1771/M2031 750,000 5/17 Sch. 52 Forms/C2118/14

Army Form C. 2118.

Instructions regarding War Diaries and Intelligence Summaries are contained in F. S. Regs., Part II. and the Staff Manual respectively. Title pages will be prepared in manuscript.

WAR DIARY
or
INTELLIGENCE SUMMARY.
(Erase heading not required.)

by [signature] Capt A.V.C.
O.C. XI Mob. Vety. Sect.

Place	Date Oct. 1918	Hour	Summary of Events and Information	Remarks and references to Appendices
HERMIES	11		Capt E. SEWELL proceeds on 14 days leave to U.K. 11/10/18 to 24/10/18 6 Sick animals admitted & 5 evacuated to No VI V.E.S.	
	12		3 Sick animals admitted, 1 Case by float. 1 Enemy Stray Horse received from M.M.P. Cpl MUMFORD, W proceeds on temporary duty to 23rd Baty R.F.A.	
RIBECOURT	13		1 Sick horse admitted 1 Mule died suffering from Wound Poll. Section moved at 11 a.m. to new billets at RIBECOURT arriving 1 P.M.	
	14		3 Sick animals and 1 Stray L.D. horse admitted. 6 Sick animals evacuated to No VI V.E.S. 1 Case by float	
	15		2 Sick animals admitted. 2 Riders issued to 3rd D.A.C. & 1 Rider issued to 2nd K.S.L.I.	
	16		2 Sick horses & 1 H.D. Stray horse admitted. 6 Sick animals evacuated to No VI V.E.S.	
	17		3 Sick horses admitted 1 L.D. Stray horse admitted. 1 L.D. horse issued to 3rd Div Signals Coy R.E. Cpl. MUMFORD, W. returns from temporary duty at 23rd Baty R.F.A.	
	18		1 Sick mule and 1 Captured German mule admitted No S/E 28929 Pte GRIFFITHS, C proceeds on 14 days leave to U.K. 18/10/18 to 31/10/18	
	19		2 Sick horses & 1 Stray Sick horse admitted. No S/E 9771 Cpl MUMFORD, W. is this day dispatched to No II Vety Hospl for a course of training with view to promotion to a Field Unit as a Vety. Sergt. 1 L.D. Horse issued to 3rd Div Signals Coy R.E.	

D. D. & L., London, E.C.
(A8004) Wt W1771/M2031 750,000 5/17 Sch. 52 Forms/C2118/14

Instructions regarding War Diaries and Intelligence Summaries are contained in F. S. Regs., Part II. and the Staff Manual respectively. Title pages will be prepared in manuscript.

III WAR DIARY or INTELLIGENCE SUMMARY.

(Erase heading not required.)

by E Sewell Capt AVC. O.C. III Mob. Vety. Sect.

Army Form C. 2118.

Place	Date Oct 1918	Hour	Summary of Events and Information	Remarks and references to Appendices
WAMBAIX	20		3 Sick L.D. horses + 2 Stray L.D. horses admitted. Section moved from RIBECOURT and arrived at new billets at WAMBAIX at 11A.M.	
	21		1 Sick horse admitted 13 Sick animals evacuated to No VI V.E.S. 1 L.D. horse issued	
BÉVILLERS	22		Section moved from WAMBAIX and arrived at new billets at BÉVILLERS at 2.30P.M.	
SOLESMES	23		9 Sick animals admitted. Section moved at 6.30P.M. from BÉVILLERS and arrived new billets at SOLESMES at 9P.M.	
	24		11 Sick animals admitted. 1 Mule issued to 2nd Div Train and one to 7th K.S.L.I.	
			7 Sick animals evacuated to No VI V.E.S. Advanced Aid Post established at ROMERIES	
	25		3 Sick animals and 1 Stray mule admitted. 9 Sick animals evacuated to No VI V.E.S. 2 L.D. horses returned to 56th Field Coy. R.E. after examination for Stomatitis. 2 Horses destroyed	
ROMERIES	26		2 Sick horses admitted. Section moved at 10 am from SOLESMES and arrived ROMERIES at 11.30 am. Capt. E. SEWELL returned from leave to U.K. Dr GARDNER reported absent from leave. Advanced Aid post established at ESCARMAIN	
	27		Section moved from ROMERIES to site on SOLESMES–ROMERIES Road. 6 Sick animals admitted. Capt E SEWELL proceeded to RUESNES under instructions from VI Corps to fetch German horses but was unable to find any	
	28		12 Sick animals admitted + 12 Evacuated to VI V.E.S. Sgt. GREEN, C reports sick and is admitted to Hospital	

D. D. & L., London, E.C.
(A8004) Wt W1771/M2031 750,000 5/17 Sch. 52 Forms/C2118/14

Instructions regarding War Diaries and Intelligence Summaries are contained in F. S. Regs., Part II. and the Staff Manual respectively. Title pages will be prepared in manuscript.

WAR DIARY or INTELLIGENCE SUMMARY.

(Erase heading not required.)

Army Form C. 2118.

by [signature] Capt AVC O.C. XI M.V.S.

Place	Date Oct 1918	Hour	Summary of Events and Information	Remarks and references to Appendices
ROMERIES	28 Cont		Pte RANGER T returns from 14 days leave to U.K. No SE/15951 Pte COLLINS, B. proceeds on 14 days leave to U.K. 30/10/18 to 13/11/18. Advanced Aid Post at ESCARMAIN withdrawn	
	29		20 Sick animals admitted 14 Evacuated to VI V.E.S. 2 L.D. Horses destroyed 1 Ride issued to 3rd Div Train.	
	30		10 Sick animals admitted 10 Evacuated to VI V.E.S.	
	31		Section moved at 10am and arrived new billets at CARNIERES at 2 P.M.	

[signature] Capt A.V.C.
O.C. XI Mob. Vety. Section

D. D. & L., London, E.C.
(A8004) Wt W1771/M2031 750,000 5/17 Sch. 52 Forms/C2118/14

XI Mobile Vety Sect. (A.V.C) 3

3rd Division

Army Form C. 2118.

WAR DIARY for November 1918
or
~~INTELLIGENCE SUMMARY.~~

(Erase heading not required.)

by Capt A.V.C.
O.C. No XI Mob Vety Sect.

Instructions regarding War Diaries and Intelligence Summaries are contained in F. S. Regs., Part II. and the Staff Manual respectively. Title pages will be prepared in manuscript.

53

Place	Date	Hour	Summary of Events and Information	Remarks and references to Appendices
CARNIERS	1		8 Sick animals Evacuated to No VI V.E.S. 1 L.D. horse destroyed suffering from Shell Wd. 2 L.D. Stray horses issued to 3rd M.G. Batn. No T/32182 Dr GARDNER, A.S.C. reports sick and is admitted into hospital.	
	2nd		1 Sick horse admitted.	
	3rd		2 Sick animals admitted.	
	4th		1 Rider received from 3rd Divn H.Q. for issue. No 28929 Pte GRIFFITHS, G. returns from leave to U.K.	
SOLESMES	5th		2 Sick horses admitted. Section moved from CARNIERS and arrived new billets at SOLESMES.	
	6th		1 L.D. horse received from 3rd M.G. Batn. suffering from shell wounds. 5 Sick animals evacuated to No VI V.E.S.	
	7th		No 28929 Pte GRIFFITHS, G reports sick and is admitted to VI Corps Rest Station	
	8th		1 H.D. horse admitted from 3rd Divn Train suffering from persistent Colic.	
	9th		2 Stray mules admitted. 1 Sick horse evacuated to VI V.E.S.	
FRASNOY	10th		6 Sick animals admitted. Section moved from SOLESMES and arrived new billets at FRASNOY at 1.30 P.M. Pte GRIFFITHS, G. returns from Corps Rest Station.	
	11th		1 Sick mule admitted. 6 Sick animals evacuated to No IV V.E.S. at LE QUESNOY. 2 Mules and 1 horse issued to C.R.A. 3rd Divn. S/Cpl FLANAGAN, R. dispatched to No IV Base Remt Depot to collect charger for 3rd Div. H.Q.	

D. D. & L., London, E.C.
(A8004) Wt W1771/M2031 750,000 5/17 Sch. 52 Forms/C2118/14

II

WAR DIARY
or
~~INTELLIGENCE SUMMARY.~~

(Erase heading not required.)

Army Form C. 2118.

Instructions regarding War Diaries and Intelligence Summaries are contained in F. S. Regs., Part II. and the Staff Manual respectively. Title pages will be prepared in manuscript.

Capt A V C O C XI Mob Vety Sect.

Place	Date	Hour	Summary of Events and Information	Remarks and references to Appendices
FRASNOY	12th		2 Sick mules admitted and 1 L.D. horse, suffering from Shell Wd, floater from 23rd Bty R.F.A.	
	13th		8 Sick animals admitted, 4 Evacuated to No IV V.E.S.	
	14th		2 Sick animals admitted, 5 Evacuated to No IV V.E.S.	
	15th		6 Sick horses admitted, 9 Evacuated to No IV V.E.S. 1 L.D. horse received for issue from 2nd D.A.C.	
	16th		1 Sick mule admitted from 2nd D.A.C. 1 L.D. Stray horse received from 2nd Divn Train.	
	17th		1 Sick horse Evacuated by motor ambulance to No IV V.E.S. Dr KENNY, A.S.C. reports for duty from 2nd Divn Train.	
SOUS-LES-BOIS	18th		Section moved from FRASNOY to new billets at SOUS-LES-BOIS. 1 Stray L.D. horse admitted. Dr JOHNSON H. A.S.C. reports sick and is admitted into hospital. No 5547 Pte SPRINGTHORPE R. A.V.C. proceeds on 14 days special leave to U.K. 21/11/18 to 5/12/18	
	19th		7 Sick animals admitted. 7 Sick evacuated.	
	20th		NOTHING to record.	
ROUSIES	21st		Section moved from SOUS-LES-BOIS to new billets at ROUSIES via MAUBEUGE. L/Cpl FLANAGAN returns from No IV Base Remount Depot with charger for H.Q. 2nd Divn.	
	22nd		2 Sick horses admitted.	
	23rd		4 Sick horses and 1 Stray L.D. horse admitted.	

D. D. & L., London, E.C.
(A8004) Wt W1771/M2031 750,000 5/17 Sch. 52 Forms/C2118/14

Instructions regarding War Diaries and Intelligence Summaries are contained in F. S. Regs., Part II. and the Staff Manual respectively. Title pages will be prepared in manuscript.

WAR DIARY for November 1918

or

~~INTELLIGENCE SUMMARY.~~

(Erase heading not required.)

by Capt A.V.C. O.C. XI Mob. Vety. Sect.

Army Form C. 2118.

Place	Date	Hour	Summary of Events and Information	Remarks and references to Appendices
ROUSIES	24th		No 15951 Pte COLLINS, B. AVC reports from 14 days leave to U.K.	
SOLRE-SUR-SAMBRE	25th		Section moved from ROUSIES and arrived at new billets at SOLRE-SUR-SAMBRE via RECQUIGNIES, MARPENT and JEUMONT	
MARBAIX	26th		Section moved from SOLRE-SUR-SAMBRE and arrived at new billets at MARBAIX via RAGNIES and GOZEE. Pte ISBELL, R. proceeds on 14 days leave to U.K. 28/11/18 to 12/12/18 Pte COLLINS, B. reports sick and is admitted into hospital	
	27th		2 Sick animals admitted.	
BIESME	28th		No 833 Cpl JONES, A. proceeds on 14 days special leave to U.K. 2/12/18 to 16/12/18. Section moved from MARBAIX to new billets at BIESME via HAM-SUR-HEURE and NALINNES.	
St GERARD	29th		Section moved from BIESME to new billets at St GERARD via SERY.	
YVOIR	30th		Section moved from St GERARD to new billets at YVOIR via BIOUL and ANNEVOIE the river MEUSE being crossed at YVOIR	

D. D. & L., London, E.C.
(A8004) Wt W1771/M2031 750,000 5/17 Sch. 52 Forms/C2118/14

V. M.V.S

14

I

11 Mob. Vety. Sec.

Army Form C. 2118.

Instructions regarding War Diaries and Intelligence Summaries are contained in F. S. Regs., Part II. and the Staff Manual respectively. Title pages will be prepared in manuscript.

WAR DIARY or INTELLIGENCE SUMMARY.

for December 1918

(Erase heading not required.)

Capt RAVC
O.C. XI Mob Vet Sec

VR 53

Place	Date	Hour	Summary of Events and Information	Remarks and references to Appendices
YVOIR	1		Routine as usual	
	2		Routine as usual	
	3		Routine as usual	
	4		Routine as usual	
DURNAL	5		Section moved from YVOIR to new billets at DURNAL via North bank of the BACQ river and CRUPET. 1 Sick horse admitted from 129 Baty R.F.A.	
TRISOGNE	6		4 Sick animals evacuated to No. VI V.E.S. Section moved from DURNAL to new billets at TRISOGNE, via LEZFONTAINE, NATOYE and EMPTINNE.	
BAILLONVILLE	7		Section moved from TRISOGNE to new billets at BAILLONVILLE via SINSIN and Bois d'HEURE.	
FRONVILLE	8		Section moved from BAILLONVILLE to new billets at FRONVILLE via NOISEUX. No. S.E. 8325 Sgt. SWAN reports for duty from No. II Vety Hospl.	
EREZEE	9		Section moved from FRONVILLE to new billets at EREZEE via HOTTON, SOY and FISENNE	
	10		2 Sick horses admitted from 23rd Bde R.F.A.	
ODEGINE	11		Section moved from EREZEE to new billets at ODEGINE via GRANDMENIL and MANHAY	
COMTE	12		Section moved from ODEGINE to COMTE via REGNÉ and HEDRONVAL	

D. D. & L., London, E.C. (A8004) Wt. W1771/M2 31 750,000 5/17 Sch. 52 Forms/C2118/14

II

WAR DIARY
or ~~INTELLIGENCE~~ SUMMARY. for December 1918 by [signature] Capt R.A.V.C. O.C. XI Mobile Vety Sect

Army Form C. 2118.

Instructions regarding War Diaries and Intelligence Summaries are contained in F. S. Regs., Part II. and the Staff Manual respectively. Title pages will be prepared in manuscript.

(Erase heading not required.)

Place	Date	Hour	Summary of Events and Information	Remarks and references to Appendices
BEHO	13		Section moved from CONTÉ to BEHO via SALMCHATEAU and BOVIGNY	
NEUNDORF	14		Section moved from BEHO to new billets at NEUNDORF. The G.O.C. 3rd Divn inspected Section at GERMAN frontier which was crossed at 10.00 hours. Route via MALINGDORF and St VITH.	
SCHONBERG	15		Section moved from NEUNDORF to new billets at SCHONBERG via St VITH and MACKENBACH	
KRONENBURG	16		Section moved from SCHONBERG to new billets at KRONENBURG via ANDLER and LOSHIEM.	
BLANKENHIEM	17		No 25929 Pte GRIFFITHS, C. R.A.V.C. reports sick and is admitted into hospital. Section moved from KRONENBURG to new billets at BLANKENHEIM via DAHLEM. No 5574 Pte SPRINGTHORP, R. returns from 14 days leave to U.K.	
MECHENICH	18		Section moved from BLANKENHEIM to new billets at MECHENICH via TONDORF and ZINGSHEIM.	
WOLLERSHEIM	19		Section moved from MECHENICH to new billets at WOLLERSHEIM via KOMMERN, FLOISDORF & BURVENICH	
KRAUTHSN	20		Section moved from WOLLERSHIEM to new billets at paper factory on NIEDERAU-DUREN road. Route via EMBKEN, FROITZHEIM SOLLER and NIEDERAU. No 17649 Pte ISBELL, R returns from 14 days leave to U.K.	
	21		1 Sick L.D. Horse admitted. No 833 Cpl JONES, A returns from 14 days special leave to U.K. D.A.V.D.S. 3rd Divn calls.	

D. D. & L., London, E.C.
(A8004) Wt. W1771/M2031 750,000 5/17 Sch. 52 Forms/C2118/14

III

Instructions regarding War Diaries and Intelligence Summaries are contained in F. S. Regs., Part II. and the Staff Manual respectively. Title pages will be prepared in manuscript.

WAR DIARY
or
~~INTELLIGENCE SUMMARY.~~ for December 1918 by

(Erase heading not required.)

Army Form C. 2118.

Capt R.A.V.C. O.C. [illegible]

Place	Date	Hour	Summary of Events and Information	Remarks and references to Appendices
KRAUTHSN	22		Routine as usual	
	23		8 Sick animals admitted. No 3726 Pte HOLLIS, W. proceeds on 14 days leave to U.K. 29/12/18 to 13/1/19	
	24		No 17669 Pte ISBELL, R reports sick and is admitted into hospital	
	25		D.A.D.V.S 3rd Divn inspects Section	
	26		18 Sick animals admitted. No 833 Cpl JONES, A reports sick and is admitted into hospital	
	27		5 Sick animals admitted. 1 case from 23rd Batty floated	
	28		1 Sick horse admitted. 10 O.Rs. attached for tempy duty with sick animals from No VI V.E.S.	
	29		3 Sick animals admitted. 1 Case floated.	
	30		8 Sick animals admitted	
	31		3 Sick animals admitted.	

D. D. & L., London, E.C. (A8004) Wt. W1771/M2731 750,000 5/17 Sch. 52 Forms/C2118/14

Army Form C. 2118.

Instructions regarding War Diaries and Intelligence Summaries are contained in F. S. Regs., Part II, and the Staff Manual respectively. Title pages will be prepared in manuscript.

WAR DIARY
or
INTELLIGENCE SUMMARY.
(Erase heading not required.)

by W. Adams Capt R.A.V.C.
O.C. XI Vety Sec.

Jan'y 1919 V8 54

Place	Date	Hour	Summary of Events and Information	Remarks and references to Appendices
DUREN	1st		Routine as usual	
	2nd		Routine as usual	
	3rd		Routine as usual	
	4th		6 Sick horses admitted 1 Case from 9th Lancers [illegible]	
	5th		7 Sick animals admitted No 20843 Pte BRYANT, S proceeds on 14 days leave to U.K. 6/1/19 to 19/1/19	
	6th		35 Sick animals evacuated to No VI V.E.S. No 17649 Pte ISBELL R returns from Hospital	
	7th		1 Horse Destroyed	
	8th		2 Horses received by Motor Ambulance from VI V.E.S collecting in BELGIUM	
	9th		No 26871 Pte BROOKER reports for duty from No II Vety Hospl. 2 Stray mules admitted. 1 Sick mule admitted from 3rd H.G. Btn	
	10th		1 Sick horse admitted	
	11th		24 Sick animals admitted	
	12th		8 Sick horses admitted. 1 Destroyed suffering from Fractured Tibia 54 Sick animals evacuated to No VI V.E.S.	
	13th		16 Sick animals admitted. Capt E. SEWELL proceeds to 3rd Division Head Quarters	

(A9175) Wt W2353/P360 600,000 12/17 D. D. & L. Sch. 52a. Forms/C2118/15

Instructions regarding War Diaries and Intelligence Summaries are contained in F. S. Regs., Part II. and the Staff Manual respectively. Title pages will be prepared in manuscript.

WAR DIARY or INTELLIGENCE SUMMARY.

(Erase heading not required.)

Army Form C. 2118.

Capt R.A.V.C. O.C. XI Mob. Vety Sect.

Place	Date	Hour	Summary of Events and Information	Remarks and references to Appendices
DUREN	14th		60 Sick animals admitted. No 21860 L/Cpl FLANAGAN, R proceeds on 14 days leave to U.K. 16/1/19 to 30/1/19.	
	15th		15 Sick animals admitted. 21 Evacuated to No VI V.E.S. Capt I. EVANS assumes command of section. 1 Horse died (Colic)	
	16th		3 Sick animals admitted	
	17th		Routine as usual	
	18th		1 Sick mule admitted. 3 Privates R.A.V.C reported for duty from No II Vety Hospl.	
	19th		1 Sick Horse admitted	
	20th		7 Sick animals admitted	
	21st		17 Sick animals evacuated to No VI V.E.S. No 516 S/S ROSS, T proceeds on 14 days leave to U.K. 23/1/19 to 6/2/19	
	22nd		3 Horses sold to Butcher. 3 Sick horses admitted	
	23rd		9 Sick Animals admitted	
	24th		3 Sick horses admitted. 12 Evacuated to No VI V.E.S.	
	25th		2 Sick horses admitted	
	26th		1 Sick horse admitted	

(A9175) Wt W2358/P360 600,000 12/17 D. D. & L. Sch. 52a. Forms/C2118/15

Instructions regarding War Diaries and Intelligence Summaries are contained in F. S. Regs., Part II. and the Staff Manual respectively. Title pages will be prepared in manuscript.

WAR DIARY
or
~~INTELLIGENCE SUMMARY.~~ by W Evans Capt R.A.V.C. OC XI M.V.S.
(*Erase heading not required.*)

Army Form C. 2118.

Place	Date	Hour	Summary of Events and Information	Remarks and references to Appendices
DUREN	27th		2 sick horses admitted	
	28th		7 sick animals admitted	
	29th		Routine as usual	
	30th		5 sick horses admitted	
	31st		25 Class "D" Animals admitted. 7 sick horses admitted 2 L.D. horses returned to 56 Coy R.E.	

(A9175) Wt W2358/P360 600,000 12/17 D. D. & L. **Sch. 52a.** Forms/C2118/15

FEBUARY. 21

①

11 Mob Vety Sec 3

Army Form C. 2118.

VOL 55

WAR DIARY
or
INTELLIGENCE SUMMARY.

(Erase heading not required.)

Instructions regarding War Diaries and Intelligence Summaries are contained in F. S. Regs., Part II. and the Staff Manual respectively. Title pages will be prepared in manuscript.

Place	Date	Hour	Summary of Events and Information	Remarks and references to Appendices
	1/2/19.		6 Class D/2 animals and 1 LD from 2nd Suffolks suffering from Mange admitted 4. R.	
			7 3 LD. received for reissue from 3rd Div HQ.	
	2nd.		3 Class D/2 horses admitted	
	3rd.		1 R suffering from Fracture Jaw. admitted from 23 Bty RFA. 3 LD from D.H.Q. for issue.	
	4th		1 LD admitted 2 mules. admitted from 3rd DAC. 7 reclassified D/2. 1 R. from 23rd Bty RFA.	
			sold to butcher 4 R's from DHQ. for issue	
	5th		35 D/2 animals. evacuated to VI VES. 1 LD Suffering from fracture Tibia sold to butcher.	
	6th.		5 Sick animals admitted	
	7th		2 D/2 horses. and 1 Sick horse admitted 2 Mules. reclassified D/2 11 sick animals.	
			& 4 LD. animals. evacuated to VI V.E.S.	
	8th		3 D/2 animals admitted 1 R from 49th Bty RFA. admitted suffering from Split	
			Pastern	
	9th		5 Sick animals. admitted 3 D/2. & 6 mange cases. evacuated to VI VES. 4 LD.	
			received from 107 Bty RFA. for reissue	
	10th		3 Sick animals admitted 1 Rider suffering from Split Pastern sold to Butcher	
			inspection of all small kit.	

(A9175) Wt W2358/P360 600,000 12/17 D. D. & L. Sch. 52a. Forms/C2118/15

(2)

Army Form C. 2118.

WAR DIARY
or
INTELLIGENCE SUMMARY.
(Erase heading not required.)

Instructions regarding War Diaries and Intelligence Summaries are contained in F. S. Regs., Part II, and the Staff Manual respectively. Title pages will be prepared in manuscript.

Place	Date	Hour	Summary of Events and Information	Remarks and references to Appendices
	11/1/19		4 LD. issued to 40 Bde RFA. 2 sick animals for reissue admitted	
	12th		15 sick animals admitted No 21860 L/Cpl Flanagan R reports from leave to UK.	
	13th		5 Sick animals suffering from Cellulitis reclassified D/2 & evacuated to VI V.E.S.	
			2 sick horses & 1 LD. horse for reissue admitted No 576 S/S Ross J. reports from leave.	
	14th		2 Sick animals admitted 1 LD horse destroyed. 6 mange cases evacuated to	
			VI VES.	
	15		2 Sick animals admitted Routine as usual.	
	16		Routine as Usual	
	17th		Inspection of billets by C.O.	
	18th		3 D/2 Mules from 3 DAC. 2 sick animals admitted 6 horses reissued to 1st R.S.F.	
	19.		Routine as Usual.	
	20th		3 sick animals & 3 D/2 animals admitted D.A.D.V.S reclassifies 16 animals D/2. 21	
			D/2 animals evacuated to VI VES.	
	21st		1 Sick horse & 42 D/2 animals admitted 42 D/2 animals evacuated to VI VES.	
	22nd		7 D/2 animals admitted 1 Rusp Mange 1 Colic (Sand) from 3rd M.G. Batt. 1 R from	
			No 3 Coy Div Train with Cows No 22622 Cpl Tucker proceeded on leave to UK.	

(A9475) Wt W2358/P360 600,000 12/17 D. D. & L. Sch 52a. Forms/C2118/15

(3)

Army Form C. 2118.

Instructions regarding War Diaries and Intelligence Summaries are contained in F. S. Regs., Part II. and the Staff Manual respectively. Title pages will be prepared in manuscript.

WAR DIARY
or
INTELLIGENCE SUMMARY.
(*Erase heading not required.*)

Place	Date	Hour	Summary of Events and Information	Remarks and references to Appendices
	23/2/19		Routine as usual with lecture by the M.O. 3rd D.A.C. (Veneral Disease).	
	24th		Captain Evans visits Coln. for the purpose to viewing new billets. 2.	
			D/2 animals admitted float for 1 HD from 3. Coy Div Train.	
	25"		Harness. Cleaning & inspection of all equipment. 26 animals addmitted & evac.	
			to VI V.E.S. 1 HD sold to butcher.	
	26"		34 animals admitted & evacuated to VI VES.	
	27th		Routine as usual.	
	28th		6 animals admitted harness & saddlerly inspection. Getting ready to move to	
			COLN. on the 1st.	

J Evans
Capt R.A.V.C.

(A9175) Wt W2358/P360 600,000 12/17 D. D. & L. Sch. 52a. Forms/C2118/15.

17 I

Instructions regarding War Diaries and Intelligence Summaries are contained in F. S. Regs., Part II, and the Staff Manual respectively. Title pages will be prepared in manuscript.

WAR DIARY for March 1919

~~INTELLIGENCE SUMMARY.~~

(Erase heading not required.)

by W. Evans Capt. R.A.V.C. O.C. XI Mobile Vety. Sect.

Army Form C. 2118.

Vol 56

Place	Date	Hour	Summary of Events and Information	Remarks and references to Appendices
KERPEN	1		Section moved from DÜREN to KERPEN	
	2		Section moved from KERPEN to DECKSTEIN (COLN) 1 Sick horse admitted.	
COLN.	3		2 Riders received from D.A.P.M. Northn. Divn. for re-issue. 1 H.D. admitted from No. I Coy Northn. Divl. Train suffering from Suspected Mange.	
	4		4 Sick Animals admitted.	
	5		4 Sick Animals admitted.	
	6		10 Sick Animals evacuated to V.E.S. 1 Admitted.	
	7		4 Sick Animals admitted.	
	8		5 Sick animals admitted. 1 L.D. horse died suffering from Calculus.	
	9		Routine as usual	
	10		1 Stray L.D. horse admitted.	
	11		1 Sick horse admitted 6 Animals evacuated to V.E.S. No. 10492 Cpl WELLS, G. RAVC and No. 17649 Pte ISBELL, R. RAVC proceed to 2nd Army Concentration Camp for demobilization.	
	12		2 Sick animals admitted.	
	13		1 Rider issued to Camp Commandant Northn. Divn.	

II

Army Form C. 2118.

Instructions regarding War Diaries and Intelligence Summaries are contained in F. S. Regs., Part II. and the Staff Manual respectively. Title pages will be prepared in manuscript.

WAR DIARY ~~or~~ for March 1919 by ~~INTELLIGENCE SUMMARY.~~

(*Erase heading not required.*)

W Evans Capt RAVC
O.C. XI Mob. Vety. Sect.

Place	Date	Hour	Summary of Events and Information	Remarks and references to Appendices
COLN	14		3 Sick animals admitted. 2 L.D. horses returned to 20th Durham Light Infantry.	
	15		1 Rider returned to 2nd Suffolks.	
	16		Routine as usual.	
	17		6 Sick animals admitted. No 22622 Cpl TUCKER, L.E. RAVC reports from 14 days leave to U.K.	
	18		1 Sick mule admitted. 7 Sick animals evacuated to V.E.S. 1 Rider sent to 2nd Army Abattoir.	
	19		1 L.D. horse sent to 2nd Army Abattoir.	
	20		Routine as usual	
	21		5 Sick animals admitted. 1 L.D. horse issued to 438 Field Coy R.E.	
	22		2 Sick animals admitted. 7 Evacuated sick to V.E.S. 1 Rider died suffering from Colic.	
	23		1 H.D. horse admitted sick. No 7589 Pte WINDUS F. RAVC proceeds, via CALAIS, on 14 days leave to U.K.	
	24		Routine as usual	
	25		Routine as usual.	

(A9175) Wt W2358/P360 600,000 12/17 D. D. & L. Sch. 52a. Forms/C2118/15

III

Instructions regarding War Diaries and Intelligence Summaries are contained in F. S. Regs., Part II, and the Staff Manual respectively. Title pages will be prepared in manuscript.

WAR DIARY for March 1919

~~INTELLIGENCE~~ SUMMARY. by. J. Evans Capt R.A.V.C

(Erase heading not required.)

O.C. XI Mob Vety Sect.

Army Form C. 2118.

Place	Date	Hour	Summary of Events and Information	Remarks and references to Appendices
COLN.	26		1 Rider returned to 9th Inf. Bde H.Q.	
	27		2 Sick animals admitted	
	28		1 Sick horse admitted 2 Sick horses sent to 2nd Army Abattoir	
	29		Ptes BOYALL, BRIERLEY, RANGER & ROOKS (RAVC) proceed to 2nd Army Concentration camp for demobilization. Authy. D.D.V.S. DM/46/19.	
	30		Saddlery inspection	
	31		No 27734 Pte RISBY, R. RAVC proceeds, via CALAIS, on 14 days leave to U.K.	

Instructions regarding War Diaries and Intelligence Summaries are contained in F. S. Regs., Part II. and the Staff Manual respectively. Title pages will be prepared in manuscript.

WAR DIARY
or
~~INTELLIGENCE~~ SUMMARY.
(Erase heading not required.)

Army Form C. 2118.

O/C XI Mobile Vety Section

Place	Date	Hour	Summary of Events and Information	Remarks and references to Appendices
Cologne	1/7/19	-	Routine as usual	DC
"	2/7/19	-	Routine as usual	DC
"	3/7/19	-	2 Sick animals admitted	DC
"	4/7/19	-	Cpl Chetmond proceeded for 14 days leave to U K 2 Sick animals admitted	DC
"	5/7/19	-	Routine as usual	DC
"	6/7/19	-	2 Sick animals admitted	DC
"	7/7/19	-	Routine as usual	DC
"	8/7/19	-	Two sick animals admitted	DC
"	9/7/19	-	Routine as usual Inspection of Section by D A D V S	DC
"	10/7/19	-	Two Sick animals admitted	DC
"	11/7/19	-	Routine as usual	DC
"	12/7/19	-	Evacuated five animals to No 5 Vety Hospital	DC
"	13/7/19	-	Routine as usual 19955 Pte Northcote proceeded for 14 days leave to U K	DC
"	14/7/19	-	Routine as usual	DC
"	15/7/19	-	No 46156 Pte Stockton 5th N F awarded 1 day C B absent from Duty from 11.30 hours until 17.00 hours. One Sick animal admitted	DC

(A9475) Wt W2358/P360 600,000 12/17 D. D. & L. Sch. 52a. Forms/C2118/15

Instructions regarding War Diaries and Intelligence Summaries are contained in F. S. Regs., Part II. and the Staff Manual respectively. Title pages will be prepared in manuscript.

WAR DIARY
or
INTELLIGENCE SUMMARY.
(*Erase heading not required.*)

6/C. XI Mobile Vety Section

Army Form C. 2118.

Place	Date	Hour	Summary of Events and Information	Remarks and references to Appendices
Cologne	16/7/19	-	2 Sick animals admitted 2 animals Evacuated to No 8 Vety Hospital	DC
"	17/7/19	-	Three sick animals admitted	DC
	18/7/19	-	Routine as usual	DC
"	19/7/19		Celebration of Peace holiday granted to all ranks as far as possible	DC
"	20/7/19		One sick animal admitted	DC
"	21/7/19		One sick animal admitted	DC
"	22/7/19		Routine as usual	DC
	23/7/19	-	No 21130 Cpl Chalmers returned from 14 days leave to U.K.	DC
	24/7/19		No 22590 Pte Marshall W proceeded on 14 days leave to U.K.	DC
	25/7/19		One sick animal admitted Inspection by D.D.V.S. Northern Division	DC
"	26/7/19		Routine as usual	DC
"	27/7/19		Three animals Evacuated to No 6. V.E.S.	DC
	28/7/19		Three sick animals admitted	DC
	29/7/19		Two sick animals admitted one animal evacuated to No 8 Vety Hospital	DC
"	30/7/19		Routine as usual	DC
	31/7/19		Four sick animals admitted No 14355 Pte Kershaw E returned from 14 days leave to U.K.	DC

(A9475) Wt W2358/P360 600,000 12/17 D. D. & L. Sch. 52a. Forms/C2118/15

D Campbell Capt R.A.V.C.
O/C XI M.V.S.

Instructions regarding War Diaries and Intelligence Summaries are contained in F. S. Regs., Part II. and the Staff Manual respectively. Title pages will be prepared in manuscript.

WAR DIARY for August
or
~~INTELLIGENCE SUMMARY.~~
(Erase heading not required.)

Army Form C. 2118.

XI Mobile Vety Sect

Place	Date	Hour	Summary of Events and Information	Remarks and references to Appendices
Cologne	1/8/19		No 21860 L/cpl. Flanagan proceeds on 14 days leave to U K	DC
"	2/8/19		D.A.D.V.S. Northern Division inspected section. Improvements to horse standing commenced	DC
"	3/8/19		Routine as usual	DC
	4/8/19		It's a holiday half the section are allowed leave.	DC
"	5/8/19		Improvements on horse standing continued, 6 balls of cement drawn from C. R.E. for this purpose	DC
"			4 "D" animals sent to XVI V.E.S. 3 horse admitted	DC
"	6/8/19		1 animals admitted. Improvements to standings continued	DC
"	7/8/19		No 34.600 Pte Fielding proceeds on 14 days leave to U.K. 4 sick animals admitted	DC
"	8/8/19		No. 22622 Sgt Tucker proceeds for 14 days leave to U.K. 2 " " "	
"	9/8/19		2 horses & 1 mule sent to Abbatoir for destruction No 45303 Pte Smith attached	
"			for training, 51st N. 7. proceeds on leave to U.K. 14 days	DC
"	10/8/19		Routine as usual.	DC
"	11/8/19		4 animals sent back to their Units	DC
"	12/8/19		D.A.D.V.S. calls & inspects Section 7 animals sent back to their Units	
"			No 23.590 Pte Marshall returns from 14 days leave to U.K. ~~S/S Parry~~	DC
"	13/8/19		~~pro~~ S/Smith Parry proceeds on 14 days leave to U.K	DC

(A9175) Wt W2358/P360 600,000 12/17 D. D. & L. Sch. 52a. Forms/C2118/13

Instructions regarding War Diaries and Intelligence Summaries are contained in F. S. Regs., Part II. and the Staff Manual respectively. Title pages will be prepared in manuscript.

WAR DIARY *for August*
or
~~INTELLIGENCE~~ SUMMARY.
(*Erase heading not required.*)

XI Mobile Vety Section

Army Form C. 2118.

Place	Date	Hour	Summary of Events and Information	Remarks and references to Appendices
Cologne	14/8/19		1 Animal admitted No 22516 Pte Page reports for duty from 24 Vety Hosp.	
"	"		Pte Livings reports for duty from 206 Emply Labour Corp	DC
"	15/8/19		Routine as usual	DC
"	16/8/19		2 animals Evacuated to No 8 Vety Hospital & 1 animal died	DC
"	17/8/19		L/cpl Flanagan reports from leave to U K 14 days	DC
"	18/8/19		Routine as usual	DC
"	19/8/19		2 sick animals admitted & 1 animal Evacuated to 8 Vety Hospital	DC
"	20/8/19		2 animals transfered to H.Q. Northern Division	DC
"	21/8/19		16 Pte of 51st Northumberland fusiliers, 4 Pte of 1/6 West Yorks & 5 Pte 1/5	
"			West Yorks were returned to their units 2 sick Animals admitted	DC
"			3 animals evacuated to No 8 Vety Hospital. 1 animal to VI. V.E.S.	DC
"	22/8/19		45254 Dr Hector. R.A.S.C. attached proceeds for leave to U.K 14 days	
"			1 sick Animal admitted	DC
"	23/8/19		1 animal transfered to Abbatoir. 2 sick Animals Admitted	DC
"	24/8/19		Routine as usual	DC
"	25/8/19		10 animals admitted	DC

(A9175) Wt W2358/P360 600,000 12/17 D. D. & L. Sch. 82a. Forms/C2118/15

Instructions regarding War Diaries and Intelligence Summaries are contained in F. S. Regs., Part II. and the Staff Manual respectively. Title pages will be prepared in manuscript.

Army Form C. 2118

WAR DIARY for August
or
~~INTELLIGENCE SUMMARY.~~
(Erase heading not required.)

XI. Mobile Vety Section

Place	Date	Hour	Summary of Events and Information	Remarks and references to Appendices
Cologne	26/8/19		9 Animals evacuated to 8. Vety Hospital	DC
"	27/8/19		2 animals Admitted	DC
"	28/8/19		6 animals Evacuated to 8 Vety Hospital. 5 to VI V.E.S.	DC
	29/8/19		14392 Sgt Horsley R.A.V.C reported for Duty from 24 Vety Hospital & Posted	
	"		to 1st Northern Brigade. 1 animal returned to unit: 3rd Batt M.G.C.	
	"		2 Animals admitted.	DC
	30/8/19		25846 S/smith Parry R.O. Reported from 14 days leave to U.K. 2 animals admitted	DC
	31/8/19		Routine as usual.	DC

D Campbell Capt - R.A.V.C.
O.C. XI Mob. Vety Section

Instructions regarding War Diaries and Intelligence Summaries are contained in F. S. Regs., Part II. and the Staff Manual respectively. Title pages will be prepared in manuscript.

WAR DIARY
or
INTELLIGENCE SUMMARY.
(Erase heading not required.)

O.C. No 11 MOBILE VETERINARY SECTION

Army Form C. 2118.

Place	Date	Hour	Summary of Events and Information	Remarks and references to Appendices
Colm	1/9/19		Pte Hearne admitted hospital	DC
			Marshall demobilised Cpl [illegible] [illegible] leave	DC
	2/9/19		[illegible] returns from leave	DC
	3/9/19		Cpl Murdoch reported from 24 Vety Hospital for duty with 70th Bde	DC
	4/9/19		Routine as usual	DC
	5/9/19		5 animals admitted & 1 evacuated	DC
	6/9/19		2	DC
	7/9/19		Cpl Rixby granted leave to [illegible]	DC
	8/9/19		2 animals admitted	DC
	9/9/19		2 .. .. 9 evacuated	DC
	10/9/19		Pte Lupton granted leave to 6.10	DC
	11/9/19		9 animals admitted 12 evacuated	DC
	12/9/19		7 .. evacuated	DC
	13/9/19		1 .. admitted	DC
	14/9/19		3	DC
	15/9/19		1	

D Campbell
Capt. [illegible] A.V.C.
XI M.V.S.

Instructions regarding War Diaries and Intelligence Summaries are contained in F. S. Regs., Part II. and the Staff Manual respectively. Title pages will be prepared in manuscript.

WAR DIARY
or
INTELLIGENCE SUMMARY.
(Erase heading not required.)

O.C. No 11 MOBILE VETERINARY SECTION —*—

Army Form C. 2118.

Place	Date	Hour	Summary of Events and Information	Remarks and references to Appendices
Coln	16/9/19		Pte Hearne [illegible] returned from hospital	[illegible]
	17/9/19		5 animals admitted, 6 evacuated	[illegible]
	18/9/19		2 " " 3 "	[illegible]
	19/9/19		8 " " 4 "	[illegible]
	20/9/19		4 " " 7 "	[illegible]
	21/9/19		1 " " 6 " [illegible] 14 days leave to UK.	[illegible]
	22/9/19		3 " "	[illegible]
	23/9/19		17 " " 21 "	[illegible]
	24/9/19		Sgt Moddy [illegible] 1/5 Bde RHA 1 Cpl Rusby XI M V S. sent for dispersal	[illegible]
	25/9/19		Routine	[illegible]
	26/9/19		"	[illegible]
	27/9/19		2 animals [illegible]	
	28/9/19		6 " D Campbell	
	29/9/19		Routine	
	30/9/19		"	

D Campbell [illegible]

Instructions regarding War Diaries and Intelligence Summaries are contained in F.S. Regs., Part II. and the Staff Manual respectively. Title pages will be prepared in manuscript.

WAR DIARY
or
~~INTELLIGENCE SUMMARY.~~
(Erase heading not required.)

Army Form C. 2118.

O.C. No 11 MOBILE VETERINARY SECTION

Place	Date	Hour	Summary of Events and Information	Remarks and references to Appendices
Colon	1/10/19		Routine	[illegible]
	2/10/19		2 animals admitted 2 evacuated	[illegible]
	3/10/19		2 " " 1 "	[illegible]
	4/10/19		1 " evacuated	[illegible]
	5/10/19		Cpl [illegible] E. admitted hospital from [illegible] through [illegible]	[illegible]
	6/10/19		[illegible] animals admitted [illegible] evacuated	[illegible]
	7/10/19		Cpl [illegible] E. [illegible] from [illegible]	[illegible]
	8/10/19		2 animals admitted 2 evacuated	[illegible]
	9/10/19		2 " " 2 "	[illegible]
	10/10/19		3 " " 2 "	[illegible]
	11/10/19		1 " " 2 "	[illegible]
	12/10/19		Pte [illegible] sent to Conv. Camp for dispersal	[illegible]
	13/10/19		Cpl [illegible] " " " "	[illegible]
	14/10/19		[illegible] Butler [illegible]	
	15/10/19		Routine as usual	

[illegible] Campbell [illegible] RAVC

Instructions regarding War Diaries and Intelligence Summaries are contained in F. S. Regs., Part II. and the Staff Manual respectively. Title pages will be prepared in manuscript.

WAR DIARY
or
INTELLIGENCE SUMMARY.
(Erase heading not required.)

O.C. No 11 MOBILE VETERINARY SECTION

Army Form C. 2118.

Place	Date	Hour	Summary of Events and Information	Remarks and references to Appendices
Eola	16/10/19		Routine as usual	DC
	17/10/19		Fire in Billets. Pte Rodgers (attached) lost his kit	DC
	18/10/19		Routine as usual	DC
	19/10/19		" " "	DC
	20/10/19		Court of enquiry re fire in Billets	DC
	21/10/19		2 animals admitted 1 evacuated	DC
	22/10/19		1 " " 1 "	DC
	23/10/19		1 " " 4 transferred to 52 MVS	DC
	24/10/19		Routine	DC
	25/10/19		"	DC
	26/10/19		Capt Campbell RAVC returns from leave	DC
	27/10/19		Disbandment of XI MVS.	DC.

J Campbell Capt RAVC
O/C XI MVS.

(A9175) Wt W2358/P360 600,000 12/17 D. D. & L. Sch 52a. Forms/C2118/15

www.ingramcontent.com/pod-product-compliance
Lightning Source LLC
Chambersburg PA
CBHW080851230426
43662CB00013B/2078